The Complete Article Writer

How To Write Magazine Articles

Simon Whaley

Typeset in Garamond.

First published in 2015.

ISBN: 1502491818
ISBN-13: 9781502491817:

Other books by Simon Whaley

One Hundred Ways For A Dog To Train Its Human
One Hundred Muddy Paws For Thought
Running A Writers' Circle
Puppytalk: 50 Ways To Make Friends With Your Puppy
Fundraising For A Community Project
Best Walks In The Welsh Borders
The Little Book Of Alternative Garden Wisdom
The Bluffer's Guide To Banking
The Bluffer's Guide To Hiking
The Positively Productive Writer
The Bluffer's Guide To Dogs
Photography For Writers

www.simonwhaley.co.uk

CONTENTS

Introduction **1**

What Is An Article? 2
Why Write An Article? 5

Chapter One – Ideas **7**

Sourcing Ideas 8
Angles 11
Topical Hooks And Anniversaries 14
Broadening Ideas 17
Local Angles 18
Human Interest 18

Chapter Two - Market Analysis **21**

Finding Publications 23
You're A Writer, Not A Reader 25
The Front Cover 25
Contents Page And Editorial Contacts 29
Readership Analysis 33
Media Packs 38
Article Analysis 40
Study Several Copies 46

Chapter Three - Creating An Outline **51**

Identifying What's Relevant To Our Readership 51
Putting Them Into Order 55

Chapter Four - Article Structures **59**

Chronology 60
Numbers And Letters 61
Time 63
Journeys And Travel 64
Q&A And Interviews 67

Chapter Five - Beginnings 73

A Great, Or Startling, Statement 74
Dialogue Or Quotes 76
Scene Setting 77
An Anecdote 78
Ask A Question 78
The Topical Hook 80
Titles 81
Standfirsts 82

Chapter Six - Endings 85

Summarising The Main Point 86
Circular Structure 87
A Call To Arms 88
Dialogue And Quotes 89
Looking Forward 90

Chapter Seven - Other Page Furniture 93

Boxouts, Side Panels, And Further Info Sections 93
Contributor Biography And Photo 96

Chapter Eight - Adding Creativity To Your Non-Fiction 101

Writing In Scenes 104
Using Dialogue 109
Point Of View 113
The Writer As Primary Source 114

Chapter Nine - Editing 117

Analysing Paragraphs 117
Adverbs 119
Active And Passive Sentences 120
Pet Phrases 122
Have A Clear Message 122
Read It Aloud 124
Final Editing Points 125

Chapter Ten - Photographs **129**

Analysing The Images 130
Submitting Your Photos 133
Sourcing Photos From Elsewhere 134

Chapter Eleven – Pitching **139**

Get A Name 142
Straight To The Point 144
Draw Upon Your Outline 145
Sell Yourself 146
Keep Records 148
Chasing Up 149

Chapter Twelve – Formatting Your Text **153**

The Traditional Way 153
Paragraphing 157
Do What The Editor Says 158
Submitting Your Piece 159

Chapter Thirteen – An Example Article **163**

Uncommon Waters 165

Chapter Fourteen – Understanding Rights **175**

Copyright 176
Traditional Freelance Working 177
The Three Key Components To Rights 179
Understanding The Impact Of Rights 181
Should You Write For Free? 185

Chapter Fifteen – Keeping Records **189**

Secondary Rights 193

Chapter Sixteen – Upon Publication **197**

Getting A Copy 197
Scan It To Create An Electronic Copy 198
Compare Versions 199
Invoicing 201
Chasing For Late Payment 204

Ends **207**
About The Author **209**
Index **211**

ACKNOWLEDGMENTS

Firstly, I'd like to thank Anne and Gerry Hobbs (and the rest of their family) for all of the hard work they undertake each year delivering the fantastic Writers' Holiday: formerly at Caerleon and now at Fishguard (www.writersholiday.net). The Complete Article Writer began life as a series of eight workshops at Fishguard.

I'd also like to thank the delegates who came on those workshops, listened, tackled the exercises and asked me lots of questions.

Finally, my thanks go to Mike White for proofreading my text.

Introduction

Stand in front of the magazine shelves in any large store and the chances are you'll see hundreds, if not thousands, of publications: quarterlies, monthlies, weeklies and even the daily newspapers. Although if, like me, you're over six feet tall you may have to get down onto your hands and knees to see the publications on the bottom shelf. (Why do shops do that?) But consider this as a mere ink spot in the inkwell of publishing opportunities, for there are hundreds of thousands of publications, ranging from freebie magazines given away in supermarkets, banks and other retailers to in-house publications produced to keep staff informed in companies up and down the country.

Now, take a step back (without knocking into the shelf of magazines behind you) and reconfigure what you see before you. Don't think of them as individual publications. Instead, think of them as collections of articles. Every single article was written by someone. And tomorrow the daily newspapers need another batch of articles, next week the weeklies will need filling with new material, next month the monthlies will need a complete change of articles and in three month's time the quarterlies will need new features too.

The article market is HUGE. Don't believe me? Go to your nearest library and, in the reference section, check out *Willings Press Guide*. You'll find it comes in a couple of volumes, covering the whole world. Its primary readership is advertising companies, but if you're looking for magazines dealing with a specific subject matter (such as footballing leprechauns) then this is where you'll find it. (Footballing leprechauns may be taking the point a bit too far here, but you get my drift.) In fact, just a couple of hours browsing through the Willings Press Guide can be some of the best time spent. These volumes prove that what your nearest news-store carries on its shelves is merely a snapshot of what's available out there.

So, the article market is vast. Yes, there are some publications that are easier to break into than others, and this book will show you how to assess that. Having said that, if you have the perfect idea for a particular magazine's readership no editor worth their salary will dismiss you. Of course, you may need to work harder to get them to consider your idea, but don't let the glossiness, or the celebrity-named writers, put you off from approaching them.

Writing articles is one of the easiest ways to break into print. If you want to get a novel published you have to write at least 80,000 words before you can even begin approaching editors or agents. You can sell a non-fiction book idea to a publisher with the first 5,000 words, but you still need to write another 45,000 words before you get close to seeing the finished published product. For both of these you could be looking at a couple of years between starting to write the book and holding the printed copy in your hands.

Articles are quicker. Submit your work to a monthly publication and it may appear in print within eight weeks. Weekly publications can use material quicker, dailies even sooner. But you need to time your submissions appropriately.

You don't need a degree in media studies to write an article. You just need to be knowledgeable in the subject matter you're writing about. And, believe it or not, we're all experts in something, even if it is the ten best things to do on a lazy Sunday afternoon in your pyjamas.

What Is An Article?

Firstly, an article is a piece of non-fiction. It's not a short story, although, confusingly, some sections of the media do refer to non-fiction pieces as a *news story*. Whilst it is possible to be creative with non-fiction, an article draws upon real life. It deals with truth and facts.

Sometimes you may come across the term *feature*. Both

terms are often used interchangeably, although in some areas of the media the article is seen as the main body of text, whilst a feature includes everything else that accompanies it, such as photos and further information sections, like contact information, website addresses and useful telephone numbers.

There's no hard-and-fast rule about how long an article should be. Those who've been writing articles for many years moan that they're getting shorter (the articles, that is, not the writers). A publication that used 1500-word pieces ten years ago may now only use 1,000-word pieces, or even 800-words. That's not to say that publications don't accept longer articles. Many do. Some history magazines, for example, use pieces of up to 5,000 words. Yet there are many other publications that only use articles of 600 words. It's not all about space either. A magazine might prefer 900 words for their one-page articles, but only want 1200 words for their two-page (double-page spread) pieces. (It's because they may use more photos for a double-page spread.)

In this book I'm discussing writing primarily for the magazine market, however, newspapers use articles too. Indeed, some of my own articles have appeared in the national press. (Be warned of newspaper photographers who turn up with a wide-angle lens. Whilst it didn't distort my text, when the piece was published my eyes kept being drawn to the photo of myself and the way my forehead appeared to curve into the centre of the photo.) However, articles differ from journalistic news reporting because they have a different structure. Read a newspaper story and you'll see that the journalist tries to answer the six key journalistic questions in the first two sentences. Those six journalistic questions are:

- Who?
- What?
- Why?
- Where?

- When?
- How?

Mark Smith was triumphant yesterday when he was first to cross the finish line in London's inaugural fancy-dress-only marathon, in a time of five hours 32 minutes and seven seconds, helping him raise over £5,000 for charity.

That one sentence tells the reader a lot of information. Essentially, it encapsulates the whole story. What then follows expands further upon that information. That's because, when space is short in a newspaper and a sub-editor has to cut some text, a news piece is always cut from the bottom upwards, ensuring the reader doesn't lose any of the vital information. If a newspaper devotes the first five pages to news stories, and it needs to slot in another news story onto those pages then cuts will be made to the existing stories on those pages.

With an article, although an editor may tweak a piece to cut it by a few words, if something urgent crops up and the space is needed for something else, generally-speaking the whole article will be cut … and, hopefully, postponed for use in a future issue. Because of this, an article doesn't have to begin with a journalistic opening. This gives article writers more freedom and creativity.

We don't read newspaper stories and magazine articles in the same way. When we read the news we read the first two or three sentences to grab the key information, and if the piece is of interest we'll read on. If not, we move onto another news story. This makes it possible to get a good snapshot of the world's events, within a matter of minutes, simply by reading the opening sentences of each news story.

An article, on the other hand, is usually designed to be read at a more leisurely pace. Readers take time out to sit down and consume articles, perhaps as part of a tea break, or to help them relax on the train or bus journey home after a strenuous day at work, or when sitting out in the garden. As a result, article readers are looking to be entertained. And that's how I look at articles. Whereas journalistic news stories are there to inform, articles have two roles to fulfil: to inform and to entertain.

Why Write An Article?

So why do I write articles? Well, for a start, it's one of the ways I earn my living. Having to generate an income is certainly a good motivator when I sit down at my desk each morning. But there are other reasons too. I think many writers enjoy sharing knowledge and experiences. An article is a great way of helping others.

Travel writers want to share the wonderful places they've experienced with others. Once you've been somewhere you've picked up lots of tips and advice, as well as made a few mistakes along the way. (Don't hire a self-catering holiday property with a spiral staircase when you have a dog that insists on sleeping in the same room as you. Highly polished wooden steps that go around in circles are a dog's worst nightmare, and an owner's too, when you see the damage a dog's claws can do to those highly polished treads.) Still, as I say, the mistakes we make are also learning opportunities for readers to draw upon, should we decide to own up to the errors of our ways.

People write articles to share other experiences too, both good and bad. Some people like to write about the bad things that have happened in their life in the hope that some good will come from their experience. Readers love human interest stories, even if it is just from the point of view of *there, but for the grace of God, go I*!

We grow by sharing knowledge. If you have some information you think others may benefit from then put it down in an article. The chances are there's a magazine with a readership who will appreciate it. One of my first illustrated articles was called *Freshen Up Your Fishpond* and gave readers advice in ten easy steps about how to clean out their garden fishpond. It was one of those annual events we did as a family during the Easter school holidays. Over the years we'd refined our process, and so the article offered readers an opportunity to learn our successful method, rather than waste several years getting to the stage that we'd eventually arrived at.

The eagle-eyed amongst you will have spotted that I've used the word *experience* a few times in this section. That's because if you've experienced something you have knowledge of it. If you've experienced it lots of times then you'll have gathered lots of information about it, which means you're an expert. If you've raised one-horned, long-haired goats for six years on a remote Scottish island then the chances are there isn't much about raising one-horned, long-haired goats you don't know. Hooray! That makes you a one-horned, long-haired goat-raising expert.

Some people write articles because it helps raise their professional profile. When you're known as an expert on a subject editors may come to you asking you to write an article for them. When you've had several of your articles published your thoughts may then turn to producing something longer, such as a non-fiction book. Publishers look more favourably upon writers who've already had some articles published on the topic they're writing about.

Then there are the people who just enjoy writing, many of whom enjoyed essay writing at school. Articles can help fulfil that need to write something relatively short, that still has some point to it.

Articles can be a quick way into print. They can help you share your knowledge with others who are eager to learn, and they can help you share your experiences. They can produce a useful income stream, if you write them regularly, and they can turn you into a mini-expert. They can also be the stepping stone to bigger projects, such as books.

So, what are you waiting for? Oh, yes! That's right. First of all, we need an idea …

Chapter One

Ideas

Nnnnggggg! Ideas. Don't you just hate them? Or perhaps you love them? Ideas are those pesky little things that have a habit of biting you at the most inopportune moment and then buzzing off into the ether, if you don't swat them hard enough and imprint them into some sort of permanent format. The old adage about writers carrying a notebook around with them at all times is certainly a valid one, but don't restrict yourself to pen and paper. A smartphone, or tablet with a note-taking application works just as well. The whole point of the exercise is capturing them for future reference.

If you're going down the electronic notebook route, look for apps that you can download onto all of your electronic devices and will sync the data seamlessly between them. Products, such as *Evernote* (www.evernote.com), let you create virtual notebooks where you can capture an idea on your smartphone, while you're out and about, and then when you get back home you'll find the idea has also found its way onto your desktop/laptop/tablet. Seeing as most of us can't leave home without our smartphones it seems a sensible solution for writers to consider.

Of course, it's all well and good having a method of capturing our ideas, but we need the little blighters to show up from time to time. And if you're looking to generate a useful income stream from articles then they need to turn up on a regular basis. The trick is to think of yourself as a great explorer, rather than an armchair traveller. Don't expect the ideas to come to you; you need to go out and find them. It's not necessary to travel to the ends of the earth though. Ideas are everywhere, once you start looking.

Sourcing Ideas

I mentioned earlier about experience. We all have experience, and this can form the basis of many of our ideas. Spend five minutes jotting down your:

- work experience - and list all of your jobs, including the paper-round you had when you were 13,
- hobbies,
- travel memories,
- health episodes,
- family experiences,
- and memorable social events.

This is just the start, but it's amazing what this process can reveal. And, if your memory is not that great then sit down with a cup of tea (or something a little stronger, if you prefer, but if you do this regularly it could explain the memory problems) and go through the family photos. (That's another good tip; photos are great idea generators.)

I used to work for a high street bank. (Please don't hold it against me.) As a result, I've used that knowledge to write articles about looking after your money and how to protect your personal data. I spent several years working for a local authority dealing with grants and European funding (yawn), but I used my knowledge and experience to write a book on the subject. My hobbies include walking, which means I've discovered lots of interesting places to go hiking, which is why I've regularly contributed to magazines like *Country Walking* and *Lakeland Walker*, and I even had a walking column in a local county magazine for over six years. (I've also written walking books too, so when I say that if you write enough articles you'll soon have enough material for a book, I really do mean it.)

I love exploring Britain, and have discovered some wonderful places, so one of my other pet topics is British travel. I've written travel articles for a variety of magazines in the UK, but also the USA, too. Think about it; if you wanted advice on a foreign destination, who would you trust more: the staff writer who researched everything online, or the writer who actually lives there and knows the place? We all know some interesting facts about our home town or village, and those in themselves can become the basis of an article idea.

It's possible to find ideas in the more mundane areas of life. "I have two small children under five," someone once said to me in a workshop. "Going anywhere, or doing anything with them can be a complete nightmare, so what do I write about?" Easy. Write about what you do know:

- What techniques/tips have you created to help make taking the children out shopping as easy as possible? What time of day or day of the week is quietest in the supermarkets?
- Which are your favourite free places to take the children out to? (Children's play area, library, interactive museum, local park.)
- Which shops have the best baby-changing facilities - national chains, or local independent retailers?
- What are your five top distraction techniques, for when the children are misbehaving?
- How do you make the most of the time when your children are asleep?

With ideas, it's not just about what you know, but what others may be interested to know. It's a struggle bringing up children on your own, but you know you're not the only one doing it. Perhaps your coping techniques and strategies could work for someone else.

Another useful tip is to use ideas you see in other magazines. Don't copy the information (that's plagiarism), but why not adapt the idea? If you spot a writer has written an article called *48 Hours in New York*, perhaps you could write a similar *48 Hours* piece about a city you know well?

At this point, though, we're simply looking to collect some general ideas. Once we have those, then it's possible to start working on and developing them. The first ideas we have are usually too vague. They need to be fine tuned. Article ideas fail because:

- They don't have enough depth to them. *Save money by always buying BOGOF (Buy One Get One Free) products with long use-by dates* is not an article idea, it's a tip. It would work well on a filler page of household tips, but does not work as an idea for an 800-word article. (What else is there to say?) However, *Eight Ways To Make Your Money Go Further* (of which the BOGOF is one element) could work as an article idea, because there is more to say.
- It's an anecdote. We all have those stories of funny things that happened to us while on holiday, or while we were doing some DIY on the house. It's the sort of thing you tell your friends at the pub or over coffee. Think about what the reader will learn from it. Will they gain anything useful from it? (Apart from the fact that you're not to be trusted with a hammer and some six-inch nails.)
- It's too big an idea. Some ideas are too enormous to do them justice in article format. A complete account of World War Two would fill several books. It's not possible to do it justice as an article.

Before you start panicking, there are several techniques you can use to focus your idea and make it more suitable for an article. The more you do this, the easier you'll find it to create more ideas. First of all, let's start with a general idea:

Fishguard for Tourists

Fishguard is a small town on the west coast of Wales, and the adjacent town of Goodwick is where the ferries and catamarans depart on their crossings to Rosslare, in Ireland. I'm sure many writers would be capable of writing a general interest piece about what to see and do in Fishguard, but if you scrutinise your idea it's possible to develop a whole range of different articles from this one general idea. Let's take a look at how …

Angles

When you angle an idea, you're narrowing in on a smaller element of it. This means thinking about a specific type of readership, which we'll learn more about when we investigate market analysis.

It's extremely tempting, when you've done lots of research and discovered a wealth of interesting facts about a particular subject matter, to want to include everything you've unearthed in your article. When you angle an idea, it forces you to choose which facts to include and which ones to leave out. What you *leave out* of your article is just as important as what you *put in*.

Let's look at some different angles we can put on our *Fishguard for Tourists* idea. For a start, tourists come in all shapes and sizes, depending upon how much ice-cream they've eaten. But it's something to consider, because not every tourist will want to do the same touristy things at a visitor destination:

- *Fishguard for the Under Fives* - now here's an angle that focuses squarely on young children. (Actually, it's targeting the parents of young children, because they'll be the ones reading the article.) But, an article about all the things that might interest Under Fives visiting Fishguard might include the Ocean Lab tourist attraction, which takes children on an imaginary journey underwater to a time when prehistoric creatures swam in the seas off the harbour. The article might also mention the best place to go for a couple of hours on the beach, where there are good changing facilities, that are safe and secure. And this beach might just be perfect for those wanting to watch the big ferries coming and going into port, too.

- *Fishguard - The Last Invasion of Britain* - 1797 was the last time foreign troops landed on British soil with the intent of invading and taking over the country. There's also a comical element to this story, because fourteen of the invading French troops were captured by a local Welsh woman, Jemima Nicholas. It is believed the French mistook her traditional red and black Welsh dress as the uniform of the British Redcoats. This angle could take the reader on a tour around Fishguard, stopping off at the key historical points in town (one of which includes a pub).
- *Fishguard in Stitches* - while connected to the above angle, it could be tackled as an angle on its own, because in 1997, to commemorate the 200th anniversary of the invasion, a Fishguard Tapestry was created, depicting the historical events in the same illustrative way as the Bayeux Tapestry depicts the Norman Invasion and the Battle of Hastings. An article exploring how the tapestry was created, perhaps interviewing some of the people who helped create it, as well as identifying the different sewing techniques, threads and materials used to create the tapestry, might be of interest to a craft magazine, or a history magazine.
- *Fishguard on Film* - The older and original harbour at Lower Fishguard was used as Dylan Thomas' *Llareggub* in the 1972 film version of *Under Milk Wood,* starring Richard Burton and Elizabeth Taylor (who also stayed locally in the Fishguard Bay Hotel). In 1955, *Moby Dick* was filmed in the area, and in 2003

some scenes of *I'll Sleep When I'm Dead* (starring Clive Owen) were filmed in one of the town's pubs. So here's an article aimed at film buffs and perhaps one of the film magazines.

Now that's just four quick ideas that came to mind as I considered this general idea of *Fishguard for Tourists*, but can you see how each one of these is completely different to the other three? So, immediately, we have four completely different articles to write here. That's four articles from that one idea … and that's without too much thinking.

Each of these ideas is looking at a narrow aspect of our overall *Fishguard* idea. But it highlights how, if we were to write up all four of them, there is information that we would use in some, but not all of the articles. For example, the Ocean Lab tourist attraction would be mentioned in the children's piece but not in the other three articles. We might mention in the *Last Invasion of Britain* idea that there is a tapestry depicting the event, but that may only extend to a paragraph or two at the end of the piece, whereas in the *Fishguard in Stitches* piece the whole article would be focused on the tapestry. But the tapestry and invasion may not even be mentioned in the *Fishguard on Film* article.

If I'm stuck for angles, sometimes I look at it from a different perspective. I might pick up a magazine and ask myself the question: *what aspect of this topic would this particular readership be interested in?* So, if I picked up a copy of *Country Walking* magazine and asked that question the answer would probably be: great places to walk around Fishguard. And there's our fifth angle and article.

Finding an angle is all about narrowing the focus of your subject matter, and it can be a great way to generate even more article ideas from a particular subject matter.

Topical Hooks And Anniversaries

When it comes to ideas, timing can be everything. The production schedule of a magazine can extend to weeks or months, which means that editors are often working on an issue months before it actually appears on the shelves. If you think about it, there's quite a lot to putting a magazine together. Not only do you have to have all the articles and photos in place, but all the advertising space needs to be sold and artwork submitted, and everything needs to be checked. Once that's happened, then it can be sent to the printers for them to print however many thousands of copies need printing, and then it needs to be distributed across the country and copies sent out to subscribers. That's not something that all takes place during afternoon tea on a Tuesday.

Editors often work three months ahead on monthly publications and anything between four and eight weeks ahead on weekly issues. So that means in the middle of a boiling hot August afternoon an editor of a monthly magazine could be thinking about what to put in their November edition. It is not unheard of for some monthly magazines to start contemplating their Christmas issues in June.

Because they work so far ahead, magazines put a lot of work into making their issues as relevant to their publication date as possible. That way, when the reader comes to sit down and read it they feel they're reading something up-to-date and relevant, not something that was put together more than three months ago.

Anniversaries and topical hooks can be a great way to tweak your idea and make it more interesting to an editor. From an article writer's point of view, a topical piece forces an editor to use the piece in a specific issue (if they like it and want to buy it). Write a general piece that is not time-relevant and the editor might hold on to it for when another writer lets them down at the last minute and they need an article to fill the space quickly (something that might not happen for years). Write an article with a February theme and if the editor accepts it they're pretty much forced to use it in the February issue (although there's no guarantee *which* February issue they might use it in).

Articles with an anniversary hook are great to write because they can be written many months in advance. They do take some planning though, because the stronger the anniversary, the more interest an editor may have in the idea. For example, the last invasion of Britain took place between 22nd and 24th February 1797. The 250th anniversary of this event will be in 2047, so put it in your diaries. Nice anniversary numbers are 25, 50, 75, 100, and so on.

But if the approaching anniversary is not a nice round number, don't be put off. Sometimes editors will consider any anniversary if the idea is right. I once sold an article to *The Lady* about earthquakes in Britain using the third anniversary of the last big quake to hit the country.

When it comes to anniversaries, it's worth spending time considering all of the potential options. For example, if you're writing about a historical character, look at all of the date options. When were they born? When did they die? When was their first big breakthrough? If they died 78 years ago, that's not a great anniversary number, but if their big breakthrough achievement occurred 125 years ago, then use that as your anniversary hook to hang the rest of your article on. Sometimes being a writer is all about being creative with numbers.

It's also possible to give ideas a topical hook. Fishguard may be a great place to go in the summer, but most people wouldn't consider going there out of the tourist season, say in November. *Fishguard in November* could be a new article idea. The area is rich in wildlife, so perhaps November is a great time for spotting wildlife, when the coastline isn't packed with tourists. (Late autumn and early winter is a good time to look for baby seals.)

Getting the topical hook to an idea right can make the difference between acceptance and rejection. I regularly contribute to the *Great Days Out* section in *BBC Countryfile* magazine, and the editor emails frequently asking contributors to pitch ideas on certain themes. Once such theme was late summer walks. As a theme, that's quite broad, so it took some time to find a walk that I thought would be of interest to the editor and ultimately its readers. In the end, I pitched an idea about a monument in my home county called *Flounders' Folly*.

My idea was a walking route that included a stop at that folly. Firstly, it's a lovely walk at any time of year, although in late summer it's better because of the flowers and butterflies than can be experienced along the route. The folly is managed by a group of volunteers, which means that it is only open about a dozen times a year. However, towards the end of summer it's open a couple of times over the late bank holiday weekend, and then again a couple more times a few weeks later as part of a heritage weekend event. This means that for the period when this particular issue would be out in the shops the folly would be open on five occasions. There was my topical hook. So, not only was it a great time to enjoy the flora and fauna of this walk, but the issue it would appear in matched the same period that offered the best access to the folly than any other time of year.

Either steer clear of the obvious topical hooks, such as Christmas, Valentine's Day, Easter, Halloween, Mother's Day, Father's Day and the school holidays, because everyone else is writing about them, or make your ideas really different to everyone else's. Looking for the more obscure topical hooks makes your ideas stand out. Sometimes those marketing campaigns, or charity/health awareness events can be really useful. Did you know the 4th January is World Braille Day, or that the 13th August is International Left Handers Day? November is when National Anti-Bullying week takes place, as does National Adoption Week. If you're writing about a specific topic it's worth searching the Internet to find out if there is an awareness week, or day of celebration that you can use to give your idea some topical interest.

Broadening Ideas

Sometimes it's possible to generate a different idea by broadening it out to encompass a wider picture. I've already mentioned that Fishguard is a ferry terminal point in the Wales to Ireland crossing, but it's not the only such crossing in the UK. It's possible to get to Ireland from Holyhead, in North Wales, and also to Northern Ireland from Cairnryan, in Scotland. Of those three crossing points, Holyhead has the better road links. The Holyhead Ferry Terminal is about 800 metres from a dual carriageway, whereas Fishguard is some 57km from the nearest dual carriageway and Cairnryan is over 150km from a decent stretch of two-laned road. So you could broaden the Fishguard idea and examine why Holyhead has the better transport links of the three places. You could simply consider the Welsh ferry ports and ask the question: why did Holyhead win and Fishguard lose out?

Broadening your scope works with other ideas too. Instead of writing about *Fishguard on Film*, why not the *Ten Most popular UK Film Locations*? We know from our *Fishguard in Stitches* angle that there are two tapestries depicting battles (Fishguard's, and Bayeux's), so are there any others? (A quick search on the Internet reveals there are.) So, why do people feel the need to commemorate war in this way? What are the ten top war tapestries of the world? And you don't have to stop at this world. One of the Internet results returned mentioned a tapestry depicting key battle scenes from the *Star Wars* films, which, as everyone knows, took place in a galaxy far, far away …

Local Angles

Having considered a galaxy far, far away, don't ignore what's on your own doorstep. Local county magazines and local newspapers all need articles, and the strongest element for these ideas must be the local angle. Can you take a national story, or idea, and give it a local twist? Remember my article about earthquakes in Britain that I wrote for *The Lady*? Well, in my research I discovered that one of the UK's biggest quakes caused damage to buildings in Derby. So, by focusing on that local angle, I sold an article to *Derbyshire Life* magazine about earthquakes.

Although I used a bit of information about British earthquakes in general, I included everything I could find about their impact upon Derbyshire. Local readers are interested in local issues. They don't really care about what's happening in the county next door. They just want to know what's relevant to their local area. Using a local angle is no different to any other angled piece: you draw upon the information that's relevant to that local readership and discard the rest. So in the Derbyshire earthquake piece I didn't mention anything about the big earthquakes in Cumbria, or Shropshire, because those readers wouldn't be so interested in those areas. (But that didn't stop me writing articles about earthquakes for those local county publications.) See? Find an angle and the article ideas start multiplying.

Human Interest

We're right nosey parkers, aren't we? I'm talking about humans in general here, not just writers per se, although by nature perhaps we're a little bit more nosey than everyone else. (Well, how else are we supposed to find these ideas if we don't go looking for them?)

People like finding out about other people. We're interested in other people's lives. That's why there are so many celebrity magazines and true life magazines full of readers' stories. We want to know about other people, and that means a human interest angle can produce a great article idea.

Let's go back to Fishguard, seeing as it has served us so well so far. There are hundreds, if not thousands, of human interest stories there. In fact, with a population of about 5,000, you could say it has at least 5,000 human interest stories.

If you wanted to write an article about great places to go and visit in Fishguard, talking to people who've recently moved there could add a fresh angle to your idea. Where do they take visitors who come to stay with them? Where do they enjoy spending their free time? What was it about the local area that encouraged them to move to the area? *Mr & Mrs Smith loved Fishguard so much they moved three hundred miles to live there!* By telling readers everything that Mr and Mrs Smith love about Fishguard you're also telling them why they too should consider visiting Fishguard, if not moving there.

What's it like sailing in and out of Fishguard Harbour everyday? Chat to one of the ferry captains and you have *A Day In The Life Of …* type article, with a Fishguard and human interest angle. What about the lorry drivers who spend a lot of their working week trekking backwards and forwards across the Irish Sea? Do they prefer the Fishguard route to the Holyhead route? (We're back to our broadened idea about why Holyhead got the better transport links. Perhaps lorry drivers prefer Fishguard because it's a quieter port.) But if you were able to interview a lorry driver who regularly travels this route you could probably get two or three different articles out of it:

- Top tips for lorry drivers using Fishguard (if the driver will share his top tips with you), for a haulage industry publication.

- Fishguard from the Ferry, a series of anecdotes about the different sights the lorry driver has seen when approaching Fishguard by ferry. (The ferries operate day and night, so what does Fishguard look like at night from the Irish Sea? What's it like getting into harbour after a rough crossing? Have there been any great wildlife sightings from the ferry?) The idea might work for a local county magazine.
- How to make the most of the ferry crossing; what top tips could the driver offer for families and tourists travelling on the ferry for the first time? This might work in a travel publication.

The other benefit of the human interest angle is the expertise that comes across. Readers see these people as experts. So readers digesting an article offering advice about how to make the most of the ferry crossing will assume the lorry driver who's crossed the Irish Sea several hundred times as part of his job will know what he's talking about.

Once you start scrutinising your ideas you'll find there are gazillions of them out there. There are some writers who say they never have enough time to write up all of the ideas they have … and this is why. Often, when you start questioning an idea and looking for the different angles, you'll see a whole range of possibilities arise. It can get confusing as to which idea to start working on first. Well, luckily, there's a solution to that. It's called knowing your target market …

Chapter Two

Market Analysis

It's at this point that many writers cry out, "But I have my idea, I just want to start writing!" That's quite understandable. After all, what more do you need, once you have your idea? Most article writers want to share their information and knowledge with other readers, so it's important to consider who those potential readers are.

When you look back at what we've discussed with regards to idea angles, you'll see that most of those angles are geared towards a specific sort of readership. *Fishguard For The Under Fives* is clearly targeting a readership of parents with children aged five or younger. (It could be argued that grandparents with grandchildren of this age could also be potential readers for this idea too.) So, for that idea to work, we need a magazine that is read by parents who have children of that age.

I also mentioned earlier that sometimes when I'm stuck for idea angles I will often pick up any magazine and ask myself: *What would these readers want to know about this topic?* Readers are the key to making the most of your ideas, and therefore it's important you know exactly which magazine you're going to be writing your article for, *before you begin writing a word of your article.*

As novices, many writers, and I include myself in this, write what we want to write and then send out our work hoping we'll interest an editor. The vast majority of times our work comes back rejected, because the material isn't suitable. Occasionally, we'll strike gold and our work will be accepted. But that's not the way to do it, unless you have plenty of time of your hands and enjoy being rejected.

When I look back at my early article successes they all have one thing in common. They were magazines I enjoyed reading as a reader. Why is this important? Because as a reader I knew the sort of material that worked well in these magazines, so my submissions were appropriately targeted. Essentially, as a regular reader, I had absorbed the style and format of the publication and knew it inside out.

However, it's not physically, or financially, possible to subscribe to every publication … and then read them from cover to cover. You'll be overwhelmed within hours because there is so much material out there. Therefore, if you have an idea that might work for a publication you haven't read before, spending ten minutes analysing the publication is never time wasted. You'll be surprised at how much you learn. When I run this as an exercise in writing workshops I only give the writers ten minutes, and it's always amazing to see how much they pick up in such a short time.

Market analysis is one of those skills that gets quicker with practise. In fact, I don't think I can look at any publication now without my brain automatically analysing it as a potential market. But that's my point. Make this a habit and it's a skill you'll be able to perform quickly, and without effort.

I do know of writers who pitch ideas to editors at publications without even looking at the magazine, and sometimes they get commissions. Sometimes. You need a lot of luck to get that right (being able to offer the right subject matter, with the right angle, to the right editor). I take the attitude that article writers are salespeople; we're selling our wares, so just like the advertisers in the pages of these magazines, it's worth putting a bit of effort into selling our wares to the right people. You can scatter your seeds over a wide area and hopefully a handful will germinate, or you can nurture them in the right environment and watch the majority of them flourish.

Finding Publications

One of the major gripes budding article writers make is that finding and getting hold of publications isn't easy, especially if you live in a rural area. You do need to tune your *publication antennae* in to every opportunity, but things are getting easier.

Seek Out Magazine Stores

Wherever you go, check out the stores selling magazines. Just like other salespeople, these stores try to stock the publications that will be of interest to their local readers, so the type of publications will vary from store to store in different areas. There are two large towns some distance from me: one is 15 miles away, the other 25. In the nearest town, the chain store stocks three tattoo magazines. In the store of the same chain at the other town, 25 miles away, I've counted more than 15 tattoo magazines. Now, personally, I was surprised there were three different publications for tattoos, but 15? This just illustrates how not all stores carry the same stock (and hints at the type of readership that exists in the town 25 miles away).

Retailers will stock local publications, such as local newspapers and county publications, so when you're in a new area, either on a day trip, holiday, or on business, pop in and browse the shelves for a couple of minutes. You never know what you might find. Railway stations are good places for browsing magazine racks, too.

Freebie Publications

Talking of railways, many long distance rail lines have their own on-board publications, often free to travellers. Pick one up when you see it. Inflight magazines are also free, so next time you step onboard leave some room in your hand luggage to take a copy away with you. In fact, you don't need to fly anywhere to get your hands on an inflight magazine. These days many are available for free because the digital app version can be downloaded onto your tablet or smartphone.

Supermarkets, retailers, banks, hotel chains all produce free publications for their customers. I stumbled across a free publication from an Investment Trust company when I was entering a competition. I didn't win the competition, but I have sold an article to the publication.

Go Digital

If the expense of buying these publications is too much (and it can add up, but remember that it is a tax deductible expense), then one way of reducing the cost is to buy the digital versions. In fact, some publications put a small sample of the current issue on their website, so you can read a couple of articles and get a feel for the publication. However, digital magazine distributors such as Zinio and PocketMags often sell single issues for a lower price than the print version. Occasionally, you'll see one-year subscription offers that are the same price as one print issue.

Another great benefit about these digital sites is that they offer access to foreign publications too, making it possible to buy magazines from all over the world. It can be a great way to break into foreign markets.

You can also buy digital back issues at the same time. And even if you don't buy any previous issues, you can often scrutinise the front covers of the past twelve months and see the main subject matters they've tackled in the last year.

Help Yourself To Other People's Recycling

Actually, it might be better to ask your neighbours if they wouldn't mind passing on the magazines they're throwing out to you first, rather than helping yourself to whatever they have in their paper recycling bins, but you get my point. Ask if you can have them after they've finished with them and then you'll put them out in the recycling.

Doctor, Dentist and Hospital Waiting Rooms

Be careful here. Not just because of the germs you might pick up, but because the magazines might be old. When you analyse a publication, always look at a recent issue, ideally the latest copy. Those in waiting rooms tend to be several months, if not several years old. Occasionally, though, you will come across publications that are only a month old, which can be really useful. Don't dismiss second-hand bookshops either, which sometimes carry a stock of back issues, but do be wary of how old they are.

When you start looking, you might be surprised at how many publications you find.

You're A Writer, Not A Reader

When you are acquiring magazines to analyse you're not looking at them as a reader, but as a writer. So don't just pick up magazines that you would like to read. *Every* publication could be a potential market for one of your ideas, which means looking at magazines outside of your comfort zone. I buy women's magazines for market research, not because I enjoy reading them. But that market research has paid off, because I have been published in them.

Whatever you do, don't dismiss a magazine, simply because its subject matter is something that doesn't interest you. You never know what you might find inside.

Once you have your hands on a publication, how do you go about analysing it? It's quite simple, really. You start at the beginning …

The Front Cover

A magazine's front cover has to convey a lot of information, because it is the main method of attracting readers' attention and getting them to buy the issue. The only readers who don't need to be attracted to buy are those who already subscribe and get their issues through the post. Because of this, some magazines have alternative front covers to differentiate the newsstand version from the subscriber version. Generally, the subscriber front cover has the publication title and a photo, but no other headlines.

The Photo

First of all, consider the front cover photograph. What does it tell you? Models who reflect the publication's average readership are frequently used. A parenting magazine for parents of children aged up to seven years will have images of young children (under 7) or photos of families with young children. A magazine targeting mature readers will have a mature cover model. A publication targeting family dog owners might have a mongrel dog on the front cover, whereas a magazine aimed at dog breeders might only use recognised dog breeds.

Front cover photos may also convey aspirations. Wedding magazines will have the perfect couple in a dream wedding location. Travel magazines use images of places that make people think, *Where's that? I must go there!* A magazine read by smallholders may carry images of people and one or two animals, but not industrial farming machinery.

Look at the front cover image and consider who it's trying to appeal to, and also, who it isn't appealing to. There are some publications where this isn't always obvious. For example, some of the women's magazines may have a young woman on the front cover, yet as you investigate the publication further you'll discover its read by a wide age range. (Indeed, some women's magazines are passed from daughter to mother, to grandmother.) Remember though, that old people know what it's like to be young, so they can identify and empathise with that readership, but young people have yet to experience life when they're older, so they don't know what it's like to be old.

The Front Cover Headlines

After the front cover image, it's the headlines that grab the passing readers' attention. Consider what these headlines are telling you about the magazine and its readers. This is what I found on the front cover of a glossy women's monthly magazine:

- Inspiration for an Indian Summer.
- Decorate with Florals and Natural Finds.
- Make the Ultimate Blackberry Jam.
- Plant a Beautiful Butterfly Bush.
- Storage Sorted: Stylish Ways To Restore Order.

I don't know about you, but I'm getting a creative feel from that lot. These are readers who care about where they live, want their home and garden to look stylish, and they want to make the most of their surroundings.

Here are some more cover headlines, from a weekly women's magazine:

- From bride to betrayed in just 10 days!
- He battered our baby because he was jealous.
- My dead girl came back to life.
- The woman who hated puppies.

I'm sure you'll have picked up this is a completely different sort of women's magazine. Here the cover headlines are sensational and scream at the reader. That's because this publication has many competitors, so the owners know their magazine will be placed next to competing titles on the same shelf. These cover headlines have to encourage the impulse buyer into picking up their title and not their competitor's title.

But these headlines also hint at the type of reader who will be interested in these subjects, so they help you build up a picture in your mind about who the publication's typical reader is.

Straplines

Look out for any strapline; this is a short statement that encapsulates the magazine and potentially its readership.

Usually, they can be found either on the front cover near the publication's title, or on its spine. Not every publication has a strapline, but I think they can be revealing. For example:

- Country Living - When Your Heart Is In The Country
- Olive (a food magazine) - Cook, Eat, Explore
- Choice (a magazine for mature readers) - Get The Most Out Of Life
- The Sunday Times Travel Magazine - Be Informed. Be Inspired. Be There.

At first glance, these might appear quite ordinary, but let's just look at them more closely. You might think that *Country Living* magazine is all about living in the country, considering its title. But look at the strapline: *When Your Heart Is In The Country*. So, these readers might love to live in the country, but where do they live at the moment? The strapline suggests the magazine is aspirational. Its readers may primarily live in towns and cities, but hope one day to move to the country. Or perhaps they have a weekend country cottage that they try to get to as often as they can. So the creative element to the articles may help city-dwelling readers create that country-living feel in their city home.

Olive magazine's strapline has changed. It used to be *Eat In. Eat Out. Eat Away*. Now, it is *Cook, Eat, Explore*, which I think follows a similar theme. It's clear from the front cover image and the contents that this is about food, but the original strapline was quite telling. *Eat In, Eat Out, Eat Away* tells you that only one third of the magazine is about cooking at home. Two thirds of the publication is about eating outside of the home, either at restaurants near home, or exploring new foods when travelling abroad. The newer strapline continues that idea, with *Cook* referring to the eating at home element, and *Eat* and *Explore* referring to the eating out aspect. What this tells you is that this readership can afford to eat out on a regular basis and indulge in food. They can afford to travel to exotic places around the world to try new tastes and experiences.

Choice is a magazine aimed at retired readers, but their strapline, *Get The Most Out Of Life*, clearly demonstrates that this readership isn't sitting in an easy chair by the fire watching telly. They're off out doing things, and so that's the sort of article they're interested in.

The Sunday Times Travel Magazine - Be Informed. Be Inspired. Be There suggests a lot of practical information. These articles will tell readers all they need to know about a destination, help inspire them to want to go and visit those places and then give them all of the practical information they need in order to get there. These readers are not armchair travellers. They want to follow in the writers' footsteps.

Straplines can also help you differentiate between magazines that appear to cover the same topics. Take *Dogs Monthly* and *Dogs Today* magazines for example. They're both about dogs, so they have the same readerships, don't they?

- *Dogs Monthly: Practical, Dependable Advice For All Dog Lovers.*
- *Dogs Today: The Ethical Pet Magazine For People Who Really Care About Dogs.*

Dogs Monthly is aimed at family dog owners who want tips and tricks on how to train their dogs and look after them properly. Dogs Today will cover similar issues, but they're also interested in the wider aspect of dog ownership.

Contents Page And Editorial Contacts

When you've studied the front cover, it's time to turn over the page. Most readers are greeted by the Contents page, giving them a more detailed run down of what's in this issue. Scrutinise it closely, because this is where you'll begin to get an idea as to whereabouts in the publication your idea may best fit.

Typically, magazines follow a similar structure:

- Contents pages,
- News pages, detailing recent events and developments,
- Features / Section areas,
- Classified adverts,
- The back page column.

In some magazines, the features area is where all the main articles are, other magazines may split their content up further into sections, such as health, travel, finance, beauty, fashion, homes, etc. But as you explore the contents pages look to see where your idea will fit in. It also shows you where you need to concentrate your interests. For example, if your idea is for a travel article, and your target publication has a travel section, then it's this section you need to scrutinise more closely. (You still need to look at the rest of the magazine, but this is the section that will be of key interest to you.)

The contents page is also where you'll usually (there's always a caveat) find the publication's contact details and staff list. Take time to study this, because it'll help you determine the right person to contact with your article idea. This is why it's important to study an up-to-date issue. You want the right person's contact name. Let's face it, you know how it feels when you get sales material from a company who has bought an out of date electoral register and sent marketing material to your home, addressed to the previous occupants. Well, editors feel the same way, you know. It's also unprofessional, and you should remember that your ideas and articles are competing against those submitted by professional writers.

If the editorial contact information is not on the contents page you'll need to keep an eye out for it as you go through the magazine. I've found them in the middle of magazines and I've also found them at the end. Some publications put the information in a font size so small even ants would have problems reading it.

As you analyse numerous markets over time you'll see that staffing numbers vary considerably, but the glossier the magazine the more staff there tends to be. This can make it a bit confusing when you're working out exactly who to approach with your idea.

Avoid *Editors-at-Large*. They often oversee more than one publication so they're not involved with the day-to-day issues of the publication. A *Commissioning Editor* is a good name to make a note of, for it is their job to commission freelance writers. Alternatively, if a magazine has several sections it may have an editor responsible for that section, so your travel article will need to go to the travel editor, your financial article to the finance editor and so on. Other useful job titles to look out for are the *Features Editor* and the *Deputy Editor*.

Don't be surprised if you only find one editor listed in the contacts section. In small-circulation publications they may be running the entire show.

Check For Freelancing Opportunities

When you go through the magazine, look at the writers' bylines, or credits, on the pages where their articles are and cross-reference these names with those on the staff list. Writers whose names do not appear on the staff list are usually freelance. This is good news, because it shows that the publication uses freelance-written material. If all of the articles are written by members of staff then the chances of breaking in will be that much more difficult.

Indeed, on the contents page you may even come across a section entitled *This Issue's Contributors*, where you'll find a photo and a short biographical note about a handful of writers in this month's issue. These contributors are usually freelance, not staff. It's another good sign that the publication uses freelance-written material.

Unsolicited/Solicited Statements

This section is also the place where you'll find the publication's policy on unsolicited material, if it has one. Again, it's often written in a font so small you'll need a magnifying glass to read it, but generally you'll find one of two statements:

- *No responsibility will be accepted for unsolicited material sent to this office, and all submissions made are at the owner's risk.*
- *No unsolicited material will be accepted or acknowledged.*

The first clause explains that if you send in a complete article to the magazine they don't promise to look after it. (And can you blame them, really? Some magazines are deluged with so much material it's easy for stuff to go missing.) What this really means is that if a writer sends in a complete article they will consider it for publication.

The second clause means you cannot send complete articles to the magazine. When you write an article in full and send it to a magazine you are sending them unsolicited material: material that hasn't been asked for. If a magazine says it does not want unsolicited material, it means you have to get them to ask for it. This is where pitching comes in. Writers will pitch an idea to an editor and if the editor likes it, they will either commission the writer to write it, or invite the writer to send it in for consideration. Once that invitation has been made the article is no longer unsolicited. So both clauses mean that freelance writers are used by the magazine, it's just that the first clause means the publication will consider complete, finished articles, whereas the second prefers to see an idea pitched first.

It's important to identify this information. The last thing you want to do is waste your time writing an article and then sending it in to a publication that doesn't want unsolicited material. There is more to pitching ideas though, which is why we'll look at this in more detail later on in the book.

Readership Analysis

We saw earlier that some ideas will be of more interest to certain types of readers than others, so we stand more chance of selling our articles if we can find a publication that attracts that sort of readership. We now need to go through the magazine and look for hints that will tell us what sort of people read a publication like this. Luckily, there are several clues we can look out for.

The Advertisements

Magazines are designed to appeal to a certain type of readership. That's because a magazine's main goal is to make money by selling advertising space. Advertisers are careful with their money and only want to advertise their products in publications that will appeal to readers who will also appreciate their products.

Therefore, to identify who the *core readership* of a publication is we need to scrutinise the adverts. Which companies are advertising in the publication and what products are they advertising?

Sadly, categorising people is how much of marketing works. When I used to work for a high street bank we were told that people tend to go through several life-stages, and their needs alter as they move from life-stage to life-stage. A newly-married couple will need a savings account so they have somewhere to save for the deposit on a house. Then a few years later they'll need a mortgage to help them buy a house. After that, when they start having children, they'll need financial products such as life insurance, should one of them die, and they ought to put some money aside for when their six-week old baby grows up and wants to go to university. And when the kids have flown the nest, they'll need savings products to make the most of the extra cash they now have from down-sizing to a smaller property, and investment products to help generate an income for when they retire.

Of course, you and I both know that real life does not run like that for everyone. But advertisers do know there are certain products that certain people need at certain times of their lives. Study the adverts in a publication and you'll be able to identify the type of reader that makes up the *core readership*. When I say *core* I mean at least two-thirds of the readership. There will always be a few readers who don't 'fit' the core readership profile. Some men do read women's magazines, for example (but they're probably just writers looking to sell article ideas).

So, what can we learn from the products being advertised to the readers?

- Who's advertising? If you flick through the pages of a travel magazine and notice that there are several adverts for budget airlines, then that's a good clue the readership doesn't have a lot of money to throw around. Perhaps the readership comprises backpackers and young people taking a year out before going to university. Which supermarket and retailer names do you see? Are they budget brands or luxury brands?
- What is being advertised? Look at the products. Who needs those products? Is Ford advertising its compact car, or its luxury executive saloon? Compact cars suggest single people, or couples, and a limited budgets, whereas luxury saloons suggest affluent readers, who've perhaps reached a time in their life when they've risen through the career ladder and can afford (and feel they deserve) the luxury. A gardening magazine with adverts for ride-on lawnmowers suggests that the readership has plenty of money - not just to buy a ride-on lawnmower, but also because they need to own enough land that requires a ride-on lawnmower in the first place.

Look at the advertisements as a whole. What do they all tell you? For example, a copy of *The People's Friend* has the following advertisements:

- Free glasses frames from an opticians for NHS customers.
- A half price, comfortable, stretch-fabric jacket in sizes 8 to 28.
- A guide to buying hearing aids.
- A floor sweeper that requires no electricity.
- Stylish, fitted trousers, with a stretchable waist in a variety of colours, from only £7.99.
- Ladies Summer Sandals - two pairs for £30.
- Reclining chairs and adjustable beds.
- Summer bulbs and pot plants.
- Walk-in showers with built-in extra-wide seats.
- A Dear Granddaughter musical box.

What image is your mind building up here of the typical reader? The adverts for the granddaughter musical box, the hearing aid guide, reclining chairs and adjustable beds suggests a more mature readership. The summer sandals and fitted trousers at those prices hint that many of these readers may be on a limited budget. The reclining chairs and adjustable beds, along with the walk-in showers point to readers not being as agile, or mobile as they once were. This might not be the best readership for your *How To Learn To Skydive* feature.

On the other hand, *Saga Magazine* has the following advertisements:

- Holiday breaks at UK hotels (with two people on bicycles),
- Cholesterol-lowering food products,
- Herbal remedies for prostate problems,

- Anti-ageing cream,
- 13-night holiday to Burma,
- Conservatories,
- Walking holidays.

The anti-ageing, cholesterol-reducing products and herbal remedy adverts here suggest a mature readership again, but there are adverts targeting both men and women, too, so this is a more mixed readership. However, despite the mature readership, there are also adverts for cycling and walking holidays and trips to the other side of the world. These readers may be mature, but they're active and off out doing things. Your *How To Learn To Skydive* idea might just work with this readership.

Inside *Country Living* are adverts for the following:

- Luxury hair care products,
- Bespoke bathroom and kitchen designers,
- Conservatories,
- Oak-framed outbuilding builders,
- Wood burners,
- Luxury bed linen.

It's easy to see that these readers have more disposable income than those of *The People's Friend.* And they'll also come from a different social-economic background. These are homeowners, and people with large properties (you should see the size of some of the conservatories being advertised here). These people can afford to have bespoke kitchens and bathrooms made. There are no adverts from large DIY chain stores offering their kitchen and bathroom units.

As I say, it can be uncomfortable pigeon-holing people in this way, but it's what advertisers do and it does reveal important clues about the readership.

Readers' Letter Page

Many magazines have a letters page where they invite readers to write in and share their views and thoughts about articles in previous issues, or things going on in their lives generally. Reading these will give you an insight into those lives, revealing what's important to them, or the things that amuse them. It will tell you where they come from. One magazine focusing on British travel had eight letters on its letters page. Two were from the UK, two were from America, one from New Zealand, two from Australia and one from South Africa. So the core readership of this publication is based overseas.

Letters that talk about funny things grandchildren do give clues as to the readers' ages, and comments from readers in a walking magazine about the six mountains they climbed in one day suggest fitness levels that many of us might dream of.

Who's written the letters? Are the writers male, or female? If it's a mixture, what's the ratio? The clues are there if you look for them.

Readers' Photos

Alongside the readers' letter page you may also see a readers' photo page, where readers are invited to send in their own snaps. A recent page in *Country Walking* magazine has eight photos, half of which were of a typical family at the top of a hill admiring the view. That typical family comprised mum, dad, two kids aged under thirteen, and a dog. Go through the magazine and you won't find articles about how to tackle the 230-mile Pennine Way in three days, because that's not what mum, dad, two kids and the dog want to do. They want to enjoy their walk.

Problem Pages

Problem pages are great because they reveal clues not just about the physical reader, but their knowledge too. Yes, there are problems we all encounter as our bodies get older, so if the problem pages are smattered with these then this can be a great clue as to the whether the readers are male or female, and roughly how old they are.

But they can also reveal a reader's level of expertise on a particular subject matter. If readers are writing in asking how to get their big end connected to the crankshaft without damaging the exhaust manifold you'll know that these are people who know their way around an engine (and that I don't, because I have no idea whether a big end goes anywhere near the crankshaft). Look at the terminology used. Is it explained, or do the readers expect other readers to understand what they're going on about? I quite like the fact that a readers' problem page can help us solve our problem of identifying who a magazine's core readers are.

Media Packs

Another useful way of learning who makes up a publication's readership is to see if the magazine has a media pack. An Internet search for the name of your target magazine and the phrase *media pack* will usually turn up something.

Media packs are what magazines supply to advertisers, telling them everything they need to know about their readership, so they can work out whether it's worth placing an advert in that publication. These packs offer useful information about the readers' age, life stage, wealth and education status, as well as circulation figures. For example, I've just searched online for the *Take a Break* magazine media pack and now know the following about its readers:

- It has a readership of 2,538,000, of which 2,116,000 are women.
- It has a circulation of 720,600 copies.
- Their target readership are women in the C1 C2 social economic background, aged 25-54, with children.
- It has a mix of real life stories, fashion, travel, food, home, health and competitions to attract that readership.

- Although they're targeting readers aged between 25 and 54, people aged from 18 to 80 actually read the publication.

The packs also contain a lot of information specifically for advertisers, about the size of the adverts the magazine accepts, and who to contact should anyone want to place an advert. (Generally, media packs only contain advertising contacts, not editorial contacts. The pack is aimed at advertisers, after all.)

It's also the magazine's sales tool at trying to attract advertisers to spend money with them, so it usually includes information to tempt the advertiser to spend money. For example, the pack reveals that 1.2 copies of *Take A Break* are sold in the UK every second, and one in 12 women in the UK read the magazine every week. Notice how the circulation is 720,600 copies, but the readership is 2,538,000. This suggests that more than three people read the same copy, which might sound strange at first, but people do pass on their magazines to other friends and family.

Socio Demographic Definitions

Did you see the bullet point about the target readership being in the C1 C2 social economic background category? This is one mechanism advertisers use to categorise readers. It uses the occupation of the main bread-winner in the family to group people as follows:

Category A - Higher managerial, administrative and professional people, such as chief executives, senior civil servants, and surgeons.

Category B - Intermediate managers, administrative and professional people like bank managers and teachers.

Category C1- Supervisory, clerical and junior management roles, such as a bank clerk or a sales person.

Category C2 - Skilled manual workers, including electricians, plumbers and carpenters.

Category D - Semi-skilled and unskilled workers.

Category E - casual labourers, unemployed people.

The reason they do this is because certain assumptions can be made about people in these categories. For example, people in the A, B, C1 and C2 categories are more likely to own their own home, because they're in better paid jobs than those in categories D and E. Those in categories A, B, and C are more likely to go away on holiday, perhaps more than once a year, than those in categories D and E. That's not to say that people in categories D and E don't have holidays, but they might not have as many, or travel as far.

Article Analysis

A media pack is aimed at potential advertisers, so they don't reveal everything about the content of the publication, apart from the main subject areas. Media packs won't tell the contact names of the editorial department, how many freelance articles they use in each issue, how long the articles are, what sort of style they're written in or whether they prefer words ending in *ise* as oppose to *ize*.

So, once you've analysed the adverts, it's time to start analysing the articles themselves.

Titles

Look at how a publication titles its articles. Are they succinct and to the point: *How To Declutter Your Home*? Or do they like alliteration, where many of the words begin with the same letter: *Seven Steps to Successful Slimming*? Or perhaps they like to use a play on words: *Natural Selection* (how to use earthy tones to decorate your home).

If you spot a trend when analysing the titles in your target publication, then try to adopt that style with your own title.

Standfirst

Does this publication use a standfirst? A standfirst is the sentence or two, usually in a larger font size, that appears between the title and the opening line. It is sometimes used to give the writer's byline (credit). For example, an article I wrote for *The People's Friend* about the Welsh coastal town of Tenby has the following standfirst:

Simon Whaley goes looking for a hidden gem in this Welsh fishing town …

In *Outdoor Photography* I wrote an article about a specific photographic location I'd stumbled across. The standfirst there was:

Captivated by a riverside spot in the heart of Snowdonia, Simon Whaley returns the following morning to photograph the location in beautiful, late morning light.

Notice how the standfirst encapsulates what the article is about. It helps to draw the reader into the article. Whenever I spot that a target publication uses a standfirst I will include one with my text. Often, the editors rewrite them completely (the same goes for titles too), but by providing one it demonstrates that I've looked at the publication and have noticed they use them. Don't get me wrong; you're not going to be rejected because you haven't included a standfirst. However, including one demonstrates to the editor that you've looked at their publication.

Article Length

How long is the article? How many words does it contain? You need to know because there's a difference between writing an 800-word article and a 1500-word article (you can go into twice as much detail with the 1500-word article).

Don't think that if you write 1500 words and the editor only needs 800 they'll cut it. They won't. Editors will simply reject your article and buy the 800-word article from the writer who did do their homework.

When you analyse a magazine you may spot that different sections of the publication require different word lengths. When I've written articles for *Country Walking* they've wanted 2,000 words plus an additional 500 words of further information panels (more of which, later). But when I write the walking route descriptions, which appear at the back of the magazine, I only have 450 words to play with. (And it can be blooming difficult summarising eight miles of route description into 450 words.)

This is why I always suggest you try to get an understanding of whereabouts in the magazine your idea best fits. Because only then can you have a better idea of how long your piece needs to be.

You don't have to count every single word in an article to work out its total word count. It's possible to guesstimate the rough length of an article by using the following calculation:

1) Count the number of words in a paragraph.
2) Divide this total by the number of lines in the paragraph. (This gives you an average number of *words per line*, and chances are it won't be a nice round number, but something going to several decimal points. Don't worry about this.)
3) You'll often see that the width of columns in a magazine article is consistent throughout the article (if not the magazine), so count the number of lines in an article and then multiply that by the average number of words per line (the answer you got in step 2.). You may even be able to reduce this step further - if the magazine spreads an article over three equally sized

> columns, then you only need to count the number of lines in one column and then multiply that figure by the three columns to get the total number of lines. Then you multiply that answer by the average number of words per line.

Your total word count figure never works out at a nice round number (because your average number of words per line figures usually goes to several decimal points). However, you'll be able to see quickly whether you need to write something of 800 words in length, or 1500 words. If you do this exercise over three articles and get results like 1,087.9654 words, and 1,143.214 words, and 1,103.914 words, then you can see that if your article is 1100 words you're going to be in the right ball park. What these figures tell you is that 800 words won't be enough, and 1500 words will be far too many.

I think word count is important because it can lead to rejection when there is nothing wrong with the writing. I'm currently looking for a new dining table and chair set, and in the shop the other day I saw an amazing set, capable of seating fourteen people around it. Made from solid oak, as were the chairs, it oozed quality and craftsmanship. It was a stunning piece of creativity. But my dining room is only big enough for a small table with four chairs around it. Any more and you can't physically get into the room. So I had to reject that fourteen-seater dining table. Not because of the quality, but because it didn't fit the space it needs to. Editors have a similar problem with words, too. Writing your articles to the right length is a good way of ensuring the editor stays interested in your writing product.

Article Style

Read through the articles and get a feel for their style. Are they written in an authoritative, informative tone, or are they humorous, light-hearted and chatty?

Which viewpoint do they use? Do they use the first person (*I did this*), the second person (*you can do this*) or the third person (*he/she did this*)? Viewpoint is important, each having their pros and cons.

First person is much more immediate. It also (usually) means the writer is an important part of the article, because you're writing about your own experience, which is why you're using the first person. (Note, it is possible to write up someone else's experience in the first person, but you're then writing it as if you were that person.) The first person draws readers into the article. *Stepping onto the balcony, I was captivated by the view before me. I couldn't wait to get out and explore.* The downside is that, handled wrongly, it can come across as though the writer is the most important aspect of this article and not the subject they're writing about.

The second person can be useful if you want to explain to readers the different things they can do, or the different options they have. *If you have a spare afternoon, check out the tapas bar on the outskirts of town.* This can come across as a friendly way of sharing your own knowledge. However, be aware that it can also come across as condescending. *If you are the sort of person who enjoys partying until the early hours of the morning you will no doubt enjoy the less-salubrious areas of town.* Immediately, this tells the reader what you think of such people, and that you don't consider yourself to be one of them.

The third person can come across as more formal. *Visitors can avail themselves of the many services onboard. Indeed, staff often overhear travellers moaning that there is so much going on they'd rather the cruise ship didn't call into ports during the trip, because they don't have the time to go off and explore.* It's a style that can create distance between reader and writer.

Look out for trends. If all the articles are in the first person and light-hearted and chatty, then you know you're going to have to write your piece in that style. If you spot some differences in style between articles, can you spot whether the editor has a preference?

Vocabulary

What do you notice about the vocabulary of the article? Light-hearted reads tend to use shorter words, whereas more authoritative pieces use longer words. Is technical terminology used? This is another useful insight into the knowledge level of the reader. Articles using jargon that is not explained assume the reader has a certain technical knowledge. Similarly, articles that explain everything assume the reader knows very little.

It's worth bearing in mind here that there are some publications that readers outgrow. Indeed, publishing companies will often produce a series of magazines on subjects at different skills levels, so that when they lose the reader from one magazine they'll gain them with another. For example, a publication targeting novice photographers will spend most of its time explaining the basics. Once the readers have learned all they can, they may then move onto an intermediate magazine, and after that a magazine that deals with the subject matter at an advanced level. While the magazine targeting beginners will lose these readers that have moved on to the intermediate level, it will gain new readers who are interested in discovering photography for the first time. The vocabulary of the articles will reflect the knowledge and skill levels of the subject matter that is appropriate for that readership.

Sentence And Paragraph Length

Don't get pedantic about this, but just consider sentence length and paragraph length. Longer sentences tend to mean longer paragraphs and vice versa. Longer sentences are more complicated, suggesting a more educated reader, or someone who has time to sit down and digest an article's contents. There's also a practical point to this too. As you flick through the pages of a magazine you'll see the article text is split into columns. The wider the column the more room there is for longer words. Narrower columns need shorter words, otherwise too many words will be hyphenated, as they are split across two lines. Editors of magazines with narrow columns will want to choose a series of shorter words, rather than have to split *antidisestablishmentarianism* four times in order to get it inside one column.

Other Page Objects
Look out for other things on the page. Do the articles have fact files, or boxouts, or further information panels (which we'll look at later on)? If so, then you need to provide something similar for your article. When I write pieces for the *Great Days Out* section of *BBC Countryfile* magazine I always have to include information about where to stay in the area, where to eat, and somewhere else to visit, which means providing postal, email, website and telephone contact information for each of these.

Article Structures
We'll consider various article structures later on, but as you flick through the pages look for trends. Do all of the articles have sub-headings? Do they all use numbered points? Again, the *BBC Countryfile Great Days Out* pieces all have between three or four sub-headings per piece (and they often use alliteration for these sub-headings too). Spot a structure like this and you'll need to include it in your submission too.

Expert Quotes
There are some magazines that like to use quotes from experts to add authority to their articles. If you notice that every article has expert quotes in it, then you know your article needs quotes too, if your piece is to stand a chance of publication.

Study Several Copies

I've seen writers' eyes glaze over when they hear about all of this analysis going on. *It's going to take me weeks to do all of this!*

they cry. Firstly, don't panic. Magazine analysis is one of those things that does take time when you first start. But the more you do it, the quicker it becomes, and you'll soon find yourself going through a magazine within five or ten minutes and getting a really good impression of the core readership and the style of the pieces. Indeed, as time goes by, the next time you find yourself flicking through some magazines in a doctor's waiting room, you'll suddenly find yourself analysing them because it's become an automatic habit.

If you can, try to study more than one issue of a magazine. Look at two or three issues side by side, because they will reveal even more information.

Templates

Magazines are often put together using templates. Turn the same pages over in two different issues of the same magazine at the same time and you'll often see the same sections appearing on the same page. The readers' letter page will be on the same page number in each issue. The main feature articles will be on the same page numbers. Heck, you may even see the same advertisements appearing on the same page numbers. The magazines are designed to sell advertising space, so the important pages will be reserved for them, leaving the remaining space for editorial. And that's why word counts are so important. If there's a page that has 800 words of text it might be because it has advertising space either side of it. The editor won't use your 1200-word piece for this slot, because that means running your text onto the adjacent page, which is used for advertising. And if the advertising department have sold that space then the editor can't use it. And taking a business eye to this situation, at the end of the day, a page of advertising brings money into the magazine, whereas a page of editorial costs the magazine money.

Once you *see* the template you'll have a far better understanding of where the freelancing opportunities are. Which brings me onto my next point.

Freelance writers have regular columns too. I have a column in *Writing Magazine*. It's called the *Business of Writing* and has a nice little logo in the top left hand corner of the double-page spread. Every month I submit my article and the editor uses it in the column. But I'm a freelance writer, so my name does not appear in the staff list on the contents page at the beginning of the magazine. So, if you were to look at one issue of the magazine you might see this section and note that my name does not appear on the staff list and therefore, correctly, assume that the piece was freelance written.

However, if you looked at a subsequent issue of the magazine you would then notice that the *Business of Writing* column in that issue was also written by me. So, although it's a freelance-written piece it's not really available for other freelance writers to send work in to. (Get off, it's my slot! Got that?) It's only by seeing several issues that you can identify where the regular columns are, and save yourself writing something for those slots. An editor is not looking for work to fill those slots, because they already have someone filling those pages for them. So scrutinising several issues will show you those slots in the publication that are written by different people in each issue. They're the sections that are really open to freelancers.

Editorial Changes

If you study more than one issue you may also pick up any changes in editorial control. Editors come and editors go, and when this happens there usually follows a change. New brooms sweep in new sections, new designs, new styles and new writers. (So, it can mean new opportunities.) This isn't always obvious from one issue. Some editors will go for a big bang approach where they drop the old format and style and suddenly switch to a new style at the next issue. Others go for a more subtle approach, changing things gradually over many, many months.

I've been a reader of *Country Walking* magazine since it launched over 25 years ago, and I've been writing for it since

2004. I've seen editors come and editors go. At the back of the magazine is the routes section where readers can find detailed route descriptions of places to go and walk in their area. These have changed as the editors have changed. They used to be in A4 format, but a new editor changed them to A5 format. Then when that editor was replaced, the new incumbent changed them back to A4 format, before they were changed again to A5 at the next editorial restructuring.

Editors like making changes so don't think of market analysis as a one-off exercise. Review your analysis of a publication at least once a year. As I've said, this is one of those skills that you get quicker at doing over time, and I don't see it as a chore, but as an opportunity. When I go through a publication and see the potential freelance-written slots I find myself thinking about which of my ideas might work in those slots. So, it's not just an exercise in getting to know the readers and the publication. It's also a way of generating more ideas.

Chapter Three

Creating An Outline

Hurrah! I hear you cry. We're finally getting down to some writing. Well, yes, we are, but don't go off and start writing your article just yet. A little thought now can go a long way into making the article writing process much easier.

An outline is useful for two reasons: writing the article, but also selling the article idea first. Later on in the book I'll discuss pitching your ideas to editors, where you sell the idea first before you go to all of the hassle of writing the article in the first place.

Think of an outline as your road map. Your article will take your reader on a journey from its introduction to its conclusion. Your outline should identify the route linking the two, and this will stop you getting side-tracked whilst you're writing it. Surprisingly, this can happen quite often, if you don't have an outline. You're busy writing away and then, suddenly, a new thought enters your head and before you know it your article has gone off at a tangent and is now tackling a completely different angle, of more interest to a completely different readership. An outline can keep you on track.

Identifying What's Relevant To Our Readership

Outlines hone our thoughts. Now we've learned so much about our target readership, it's important that we tailor the information from our idea and only use what's relevant for our target readership. This is where I go through my research and subject information, pulling out the key points that I think will be most relevant to the readership.

For example, many people, especially self-employed people, have the joy of dealing with their tax returns every year. There are steps they can take to make life more easier for this process:

- creating simple systems for recording all income and expenditure,
- identifying legitimate business expenditure items to offset against tax,
- being able to calculate your profits (income minus expenditure),
- considering whether it's necessary to be registered for VAT purposes,
- whether to consider engaging the use of an accountant,
- identifying other taxes you may be liable for: National Insurance for yourself and any employees you may have,
- claiming all allowances you're entitled to, such as uniform cleaning,
- learning about capital expenditure and allowances,
- learning about capital gains tax,
- understanding the implications of taking on employees, and the need for a pension scheme for them.

As a general idea, this could be classified as business finance, but for it to work as an article we need to have a clearly defined readership and an angle, or topical hook. The topical hook is straightforward. In the UK the new tax year starts on 6th April, so an article on this subject would work best in the April issue of a magazine. But which magazine are we targeting?

Let's look close to home. If you're looking to write articles and be paid for your work, then you're a business, trying to sell your product to an audience. That means that most writers (with the exception of those who write purely for the enjoyment it gives them) should classify themselves as self-employed business people. So let's consider approaching a magazine that is read by budding writers and offer them an article about being prepared for the taxman. Heck, there's even a title forming in my head right now. We could call our article: *Writing Shouldn't Be Taxing.*

Our readership comprises writers of all ages, some of whom may have had a couple of short stories or articles published, or perhaps some have self-published their novel, whilst others are still waiting to see their name in print. Some readers may have generated some income from their writing efforts, while others are working hard trying to get their first payment. Essentially, the core readership is hoping to be paid for their work at some point, so the subject matter is important to them. But will they be interested in all of the points we've identified in our bullet list above? Let's take a closer look.

1. creating simple systems for recording all income and expenditure, (*Yes, this is important for writers, so we need to include this.*)
2. identifying legitimate business expenditure items to offset against tax, (*Yes, writers incur certain types of expenditure that can be offset against any income to reduce their tax - things like stationery, ink, postage, subscriptions to writing magazines.*)
3. being able to calculate your profits (income minus expenditure), (*Yes, writers need to know how to do this.*)
4. considering whether it's necessary to be registered for VAT purposes, (*For our target readership VAT won't be an issue. Writers who need to register for VAT are generating a lot of business income and expenditure. That's not the readership of our target publication, so we don't need to mention this.*)
5. whether to consider engaging the use of an accountant, (*This could be something to consider, so it might be worth mentioning.*)

6. identifying other taxes you may be liable for: National Insurance for yourself and any employees you may have, (*Some of this is relevant. Self-employed writers are liable for National Insurance for themselves, but most writers don't have employees, so we can ignore the employee implications for this readership.*)
7. claiming all allowances you're entitled to, such as uniform cleaning, (*Most writers don't wear uniforms - and our pyjamas can't be classified as a uniform. Only writing-related allowances should be mentioned to this readership.*)
8. learning about capital expenditure and allowances, (*Capital expenditure relates to large items like machinery, vehicles and equipment. Writers don't tend to use much machinery, although it may be worth mentioning computers and printers, because these would be classified as capital items.*)
9. learning about capital gains tax, (*This would be outside the scope of our readership.*)
10. understanding the implications of taking on employees, and the need for a pension scheme for them. (*As most writers don't have employees, this isn't of interest to our readership.*)

Hopefully, this shows that our target readership won't be interested in everything we've researched on the subject, so we can dismiss the information that is irrelevant to this readership. We're left with the points that these specific readers will be interested in:

1. creating simple systems for recording all income and expenditure,
2. identifying legitimate business expenditure items to offset against tax,
3. being able to calculate your profits (income minus expenditure),
5. whether to consider engaging the use of an accountant,
6. identifying other taxes you may be liable for: National Insurance,

7. claiming all allowances you're entitled to,
8. learning about capital expenditure and allowances.

Of our initial ten points, only seven may be of interest to these particular readers (we've dropped points 4, 9 and 10). If we were to write an article for a different magazine with a different readership, we would probably find ourselves drawing upon different points. If writing for a magazine targeting budding restaurateurs we'd be focusing more on employee implications, because most restaurants need a team of front-of-house staff, as well as a decent chef.

Going through your information at this stage will not only help to keep you focused on your target readership, but it will also show you whether you have enough information for the length of article required for this particular market.

Putting Them Into Order

When you have your key points identified, take a look at them and consider re-arranging them into some sort of order. We're beginning to slip into the realms of article structure here, but it's a useful exercise to undertake because this structured outline can be used as part of your pitch to a magazine editor, if you want to sell them the idea first and have them commission you to write the full article.

Think about how you're going to reveal this information to the reader. Do some points need explaining first before you can discuss more complicated points? Here are the points we've decided to discuss in our tax article for writers:

1. creating simple systems for recording all income and expenditure,
2. identifying legitimate business expenditure items to offset against tax,
3. being able to calculate your profits (income minus expenditure),

5. whether to consider engaging the use of an accountant,
6. identifying other taxes you may be liable for: National Insurance,
7. claiming all allowances you're entitled to,
8. learning about capital expenditure and allowances.

When creating an article on this subject, I'd put these points into the following order:

3. being able to calculate your profits (income minus expenditure) - *I would want to explain first that writers only pay tax on any profits, so it's vital that writers know how to calculate what the profit.*
1. creating simple systems for recording all income and expenditure - *Now we know why we have to keep records of all of our income and expenditure, I would explain some simple steps we can take to ensure we capture all of this information in a straightforward manner.*
2. identifying legitimate business expenditure items to offset against tax - *Knowing we can claim certain business expenditure against any income we earn, I would then look at the legitimate expenses we need to keep track of.*
7. claiming all allowances you're entitled to - *After identifying all of our allowable expenses, I would begin to look at any special allowances writers can claim.*
8. learning about capital expenditure and allowances - *I would briefly mention capital expenditure, such as computers and printers, which have special rules relating to how they are accounted for.*
6. identifying other taxes you may be liable for: National Insurance - *After the good news of all these expenses and allowances, it's time to look at the negative side of things - what else are we liable for?*
5. whether to consider engaging the use of an accountant - *finally, I would round off with suggesting at what point in a writer's career an accountant may be required, and how to go about finding one.*

Can you see how there's some structure here? The article idea now starts off with the basics, and then progresses into more detail as we drill down into the subject matter. Creating an outline is easier with some subjects than it is with others, so don't worry too much if your subject matter could be dealt with in a variety of ways, and you're unsure how best to proceed. Sometimes, the outline becomes more obvious when you begin considering your overall article structure …

Chapter Four

Article Structures

While an outline can help you decide the *order* of the information you give to the reader, the article's structure determines *how* you give them that information. As I said earlier, sometimes there is some overlap between outline order and article structure, but when you go through your magazine analysis and study your target market you might notice that the publication has a preference for a certain type of article structure.

Alternatively, there may be a specific type of structure for a certain section of the magazine. For example, I regularly contribute walking route descriptions to *Country Walking* magazine, offering detailed walking routes that readers can follow. Now, my outline for the piece is straightforward: I present the reader with the right directions to follow in the order they need to enable them to complete the walk. The piece takes the reader from the start of the walk, point 1, to point 2, then point 3, then 4, before returning them to the start (because the magazine prefers circular walks). Each number is a key navigational point of the walk, but it may also be a great viewpoint, a place of historic interest, or a great place to see wildlife.

However, in the main section of the magazine, the articles take on different structures. On one occasion the editor commissioned me to write an article about my home town, using a *48 Hours in …* structure. (It's great when editors contact you out of the blue like that!) So, instead of telling readers which path to take and which stile to cross, this article gave readers a suggested itinerary, using key times of the day as my structure. I suggested where to set off and walk to at 9am, which pub to stop at for lunch at 1pm, and so on.

Choose the wrong structure and you could end up confusing your reader. On the other hand, the right structure can add coherence and authority to your text.

I ought to point out that when I'm talking about the article structure I'm referring to the main middle section of your article. I know, I know, I know … we haven't looked at beginnings yet, but just because everything has to have a beginning, a middle and an end, there's no law that says we have to write them in that order. I think beginnings and endings are easier to write when you've written the main middle section. (Try it at some point to see of it works for you.)

It's possible to write completely different articles on the same idea and angle (and even outline) by using different article structures. (I did say that once you had an idea you should milk it for every opportunity.) So let's take a closer look at the structures that might be of use to you …

Chronology

This is the most straightforward of structures, where you start at the beginning, and recount events as they happened, until you reach the point where you want to end. It makes sense to use this structure for historical pieces, for example. Skipping back and forth between time periods can easily confuse the reader.

This is also a common structure for the real life reader's stories that you see in many of the women's magazines. A problem is identified and then the reader recounts in chronological order the sequence of events that led to the problem's conclusion. The beauty about chronology is that it is easy for the reader to follow. Sometimes, for complicated topics, a chronological structure is the best way to convey the events in the simplest format.

You may come across a slight variation of this format, similar to that used in short stories. If you've studied short stories, you may have learned that a short story should start at a point of crisis, the resolution of which is the rest of the story. In this structure, the story begins at an exciting moment, and then may go back in time to give the reader the back story, before continuing with the tale. With the exception of the opening scene, the story is generally told in chronological order. Sometimes, this *out-of-sync opening scene* scenario can also work for articles, and you may come across it in the real-life reader stories you see (because these are frequently told in the same style as a fictional story). We'll look at beginnings in the next chapter, but it's worth bearing in mind that sometimes a chronological structure can be shaken up a bit at the start in this way.

Chronological structures are great for historical articles, readers' real-life stories, some travel pieces, and biographical articles (which can also be great anniversary articles).

Numbers And Letters

Magazines love numbers. Numbers help sell magazines, which is why you often see them on the front cover: *Ten Ways To Drop A Dress Size. Seven Successful Slimming Secrets. The Five Step Make-Up Plan. Twenty Ways To Declutter Your Home. Eight Fantastic City Destinations For A Romantic Weekend.* See what I mean? This type of cover headline often attempts to scream out to magazine browsers as they peruse the shelves. Go on. Next time you go to a shop selling magazines, just look for the numbers.

The most popular numbers are: 5, 7, 8, 10, 15, 20, 25, 50, 75 and 100, but you can use other numbers too. I've seen articles offering *Six ways* to do something, *Thirty Seven Knock Out Ways* to do something else, and one women's magazine claimed an article with *237 Wardrobe Tips.* (I don't have a wardrobe big enough, which is probably why this article was in a women's magazine and not a men's magazine.)

The great thing about a number structure is that these articles are highly-focused. You start off with point 1, discuss the topic, then move onto point 2, and so on. There's no need for any linking words or phrases to take readers from one paragraph to another. Each numbered point has its own heading. Remember the article I mentioned about cleaning out my fishpond? That was a number structure, giving readers advice on how to clean out their fishpond in ten easy steps, like so:

Step 1: Preparation Is Key
Collect all the equipment and tools needed before you start. Fish require surface area, rather than depth, so make sure your temporary fish-storage area is large enough. A children's paddling pool is perfect. Other pond life, such as newts, insects and oxygenating plants can go into deeper containers, like dustbins.

Step 2: Use What You've Got
Fill your temporary fish-storage tank with water from the pond, not from the tap. Transfer across enough oxygenating plants to provide shade, if tackling this on a hot day. Then begin the joy of trying to catch the fish.

By using each numbered point as a heading, the structure becomes clear to the reader. This means that the text underneath each numbered heading is concise and to the point. There's less chance of waffling with this sort of structure.

You may also come across a numbered structured that uses a cumulative approach. Instead of using consecutive numbers (1, 2, 3, 4, 5, and so on) it uses numbers in a way that reaches a grand total in a series of unequal steps. For example, the article idea may be to save £500 a month from your monthly household expenditure, and each point takes you from a starting point of £0 savings at the beginning of the article to £500 saved at the end of the article, like so:

Pay Your Line Rental Upfront: Total Monthly Saving = £5
Instead of paying your landline rental on a monthly basis, pay for 12 months in advance and you pay less, saving, on average £5 per month. (That's £60 a year.)

Threaten To Leave Your Pay-TV Provider: Total Monthly Saving = £65
If you're paying top whack for your monthly TV package, give your supplier a call and threaten to leave. You'll be surprised what they can do to keep you. Some readers have cut their monthly package bill by £60.

And so the article goes on, until it reaches that £500 target.

Letters provide another useful structure, although they're not as popular these days. *An A-Z of* … type article used to be common, if only for the ingenious ways writers had to deal with the troublesome letters of Q, V, X and Z. A feature offering an A to Z of a county's villages, or an A to Z of great herbs to include in your cooking, or an A to Z of sporting greats for an annual review, can work really well, however, with 26 points to make, it's perhaps only something worth considering for markets that use longer articles. To produce an equally balanced article, if you wrote a 1500-word A to Z piece you would have an average of 57 words per letter. This doesn't give you much room for detail, nor does it include anything for a beginning and an ending either.

One way to get around this is to break it up and offer an editor a series of articles, perhaps over four or five issues. But if you're really clever you may be able to sell them one letter per issue, and bag a 26-issue series of articles.

Time

Time can be a useful means of structuring an article, because it's a format that everyone can identify with. Popular time structures include:

- *A Day In The Life Of…* this focuses on the waking hours of somebody, usually looking at their professional life. You start from the moment they wake up until the time they go back to bed.

- *24 /48 hours* - often used for travel features, these give you an itinerary for either one or two days in a resort/destination. (Sleeping hours often focus on great places to kip for the night.)
- *A week* - similar to a day in the life, this will generally examine a person's working week. In some ways, it's not as intense as a day in the life piece, because you don't have to account for every waking hour, but the whole week needs to be exciting. You can't write about someone who has one really busy day and then six days of not doing much else.
- *The seasons* - it's not used very often, but a seasonal approach to a subject can offer an alternative structure. You may see travel articles alluding to the seasons: *Bruges in Spring, New England in Autumn.*
- *A year* - although this covers a long period of time in what could be a short amount of space (1,000 to 1,500-words), it does allow you to cover it in two ways: either monthly, or seasonally. It depends whether your subject matter has twelve clear points that you can allocate to each month, or whether you're better focusing on four main points with a handful of others supplementing them.

Of course, there will always be exceptions, and sometimes those make for a more interesting structure, because it's something different to what readers usually see. A wildlife article might look at the lifecycle of an animal, which might last a few hours, or extend to several years.

Journeys And Travel

Oh, the *J word!* Where would reality TV shows be without the *J word (journey)*? It gets used so much because that's what life is, and it's a structure that many articles use too. The obvious market is travel features, but almost any type of article can be written up as a journey of one form or another.

Incidentally, you may spot that some travel features mix and match article structures. For example, a *48 Hours in …* type feature uses time as the main structure, but it could also take readers on a journey from one place to another during that time period.

The journey structure needs to have a beginning, middle and an end. (Yes, in some ways, *all* articles are journeys.) The journey might involve physical travelling, such as exploring a city for the first time, or following a village trail, or the joys and tribulations of just getting to the airport. Or it could be an emotional journey, such as coming to terms with a change in your life. An article explaining how you turned redundancy into a new opportunity to completely change your life could be both a physical and an emotional journey.

For such journey pieces there needs to be a clear starting point, and a defined destination, with, hopefully, some interesting bits in the middle. For example, when my first book (*One Hundred Ways For A Dog To Train Its Human*) hit the bestseller lists, a writing magazine asked me to produce an article about it and explain how it all happened. I treated that as a journey structure: my starting point was getting the original 75-word filler published and then realising the idea had more mileage. After that I moved onto the middle section, showing how I expanded the filler into an 800-word article, and from there into a short book (while also mentioning the tribulations of having the book idea rejected by four publishers first, before I found the right one). The piece ended with me commenting about the last week the book spent on the bestseller lists. The article was several journeys in one, really. It was the main journey of idea to bestseller list, but it was also a journey about realising my writing life and dreams.

Travel features often benefit by turning them into a journey of some kind. I was commissioned to write a travel feature about Tenby, on the Pembrokeshire coast for *The People's Friend* and I'd identified the key places I wanted to mention in my article. But simply listing them as a series of great places to look out for the next time you're in Tenby meant the article didn't work. It came across as disjointed. So I turned it into a physical journey. I created a mystery and made out that the only way to solve it was to explore the town looking for clues. When readers sat down and read the article, they could have plotted the route I took around Tenby on a map and followed in my footsteps.

By doing that, it completely changed the article from an unconnected list of Tenby tourist attractions into a story with a clear destination at the end. The article set off to achieve something and the readers wanted to know if I would meet that goal.

There are generally two main types of travel readers: those who want to physically follow in your footsteps, and those who are armchair travellers - they want to feel as though they are travelling alongside you. (There is, in my opinion, a third category of travel reader: those who want to be inspired to go and explore somewhere, but want to create their own itinerary, so they're not looking for physical journeys they can follow. They merely want to be inspired about the options available so they can go off and create their own.)

A travel journey doesn't always have to be a physical journey for readers to follow. You could create a journey through time … a chronological journey. A feature about the castles of Wales could take readers on a journey back and forth across the land, moving from one castle building period to another.

I wrote an article about famous people who'd been buried in Cumbria, and because of the county's challenging terrain creating a physical journey for readers to follow wasn't possible. But I realised that a bird would have no problem flying from one place to the next, so I created a route that readers could still follow on a map, but one that would take the easiest route *as the crow flies*, as we might say. Not a typical journey, I'll grant you, but it still gave my article a journey structure, and one that enabled me to create a circular journey as well. Be creative with your journeys.

One important point I'd like to make about travel articles is that your whole trip is not one article journey, but several. Focus in on a small part of your trip, for each article. If you go to America for two weeks, your travel article does not have to follow the time structure and become *My Two Weeks In America*. Do that and you fall into the what-I-did-on-my-school-holidays type structure.

I spent a week on holiday in Pembrokeshire. The travel piece I wrote for *The People's Friend* was one afternoon of that week. On another day I did a seven-mile walk along the coast path, which became another piece for a walking magazine. And I turned several moments from throughout the holiday into an article about the quest for some bubblegum flavoured ice-cream. (The things uncles have to do for their nephews.) So, think about your trip as a series of journeys for different readerships, not one long journey for one readership.

Q&A And Interviews

There was a time when interview pieces were written as a series of questions and answers. The writer's questions often appeared in a bold typeface, with the interviewee's responses underneath. Indeed, in some publications you still see this sort of structure, often for short interviews (*Five minutes with …*)

The great thing about interviews is that one question often leads onto another, so there's a natural structure to them, as the conversation develops.

However, writing an interview in a Q&A style is quite old fashioned (although as the saying goes, what goes around comes around, so no doubt it'll come back into fashion). Interview pieces can be written in ways where the questions aren't asked directly. Instead, the writer/interviewer signals to the reader what's been asked, and allows the interviewee to provide the answer, which confirms to the reader what has been asked. What this does is it makes the interviewee the main focus of the article, and the writer steps back into the shadows a bit.

While some writers plan everything to the smallest of details, Martin Smith prefers to take a more laid back approach. "I have a rough idea of where my ending is going to be, but I don't always know how I'm going to get there. I love allowing my characters the freedom to talk and do what they want, and it always amazes me how things pan out in the end. I feel that this allows me to discover the journey in the same way that the reader does."

When you undertake a market analysis you may also come across variations of the Q&A structure. Articles that want to tackle both sides of an argument may ask the same questions to two people on opposing sides (great for political and environmental stories). Your piece may then follow a Q&A&A structure, where the question is asked, making it clear to the reader that both sides are being asked the same question, and then two answers are provided, one from each person.

Interview pieces vary in style, and when you analyse a publication try to ascertain the style that is being adopted. Who are you *aware of* in the interview? Some pieces focus purely on the interviewee. They take the attitude that it's what they say that is important. Other interviews might include observations by the writer. When you pick up phrases like, *He sits in the chair opposite, his hands in his lap, but his thumbs constantly twiddling. He makes eye contact frequently, but also glances around the room, as if he's looking for an escape route, should he need a quick exit.* Here, the writer is conveying what *they* are noticing, and so this makes them just as important to the reader as the interviewee. The writer is as much part of the interview as the interviewee, and therefore the reader is more aware of this.

These interview pieces are a different structure, because

these writer-observations are interspersed amongst the interviewee's responses. This provides a different perspective on what the interviewee is saying. If an interviewee says one thing, but their body language suggests something different, the writer is using their observations to convey more information to the reader.

Logical Sequence Articles

It's possible to use a Q&A approach when writing other articles, too. Q&As are not just for interview pieces. This type of article is sometimes referred to as the *Logical Sequence* structure. It's where the writer might choose a topic and then ask a series of questions that the typical reader might ask in order to find out more about the topic. With the questions raised the writer then sets about answering them. Imagine the topic you've chosen to write about is whether the food we eat can improve our writing productivity. You might begin listing some questions on the topic, like so:

- Can what we eat affect our creativity?
- If so, how should we start our day? What should we eat for breakfast?
- What happens if we feel peckish mid-morning? What should we snack on to remain alert?
- What's the best lunch to keep us alert and creative in the afternoon?
- How do we avoid that afternoon slump?
- What should we eat in the evenings to ensure we have a good night's sleep and wake up refreshed and raring to go the following day?

These are questions that anyone would ask, once the topic has first been raised. You might find that you need to re-arrange some of the questions, but once they're in a logical order, you can start answering them:

Can what we eat affect our creativity?

Most of us appreciate that unhealthy food affects our physical health, but sometimes we forget that a writer's most important body part, our brain, is part of that same physical body. It's where our creativity occurs and it is the third largest organ in our body, so feeding it with the right food will make it fitter, healthier, productive and more positive.

So what should we eat for breakfast?

If you're settling down to add another 5,000 words to the novel, then you need a good breakfast: one that will provide you with stamina and sustenance for several hours. This is the most important meal of the day. When the University of Bristol undertook a study of 126 volunteers, aged between 20 and 79 years old, and assessed their mental health, it was those who ate breakfast everyday who were less depressed, less stressed and had lower perceived levels of stress than those who missed breakfast.

A good brain-enhancing breakfast should include wholegrain to provide carbohydrates that slowly release energy throughout the morning. Skipping breakfast encourages stressed writers to grab sugary snacks, containing ineffective simple carbohydrates. Whilst they provide a quick energy boost, it's short-lived, unsustainable and ultimately demoralising.

What happens if we feel peckish mid-morning? What should we snack on to remain alert?

As the morning wears on, our creative productivity drops. If you're interviewing people for those all-important quotes, your brain needs to be alert to ensure you ask all the right questions. Give yourself a banana boost. Bananas contain three natural sugars: sucrose, fructose and glucose. These provide a quick energy boost and sustained energy uplift too. In addition to healthy fibre, bananas contain tryptophan, an amino acid needed by the body to produce the mood-enhancing hormone, serotonin. When released, serotonin gives a relaxing, contented feeling, relieving emotional tension. Bananas are also packed with vitamin C, B6, potassium, magnesium and folate. Researchers in India also discovered that people who ate two bananas a day for a week successfully lowered their blood pressure by 10%.

Written like this, it's as though there's an interview taking place. However, if you delete the questions, leaving just the answers, you'll see that what's left still reads as a well-structured article, because it's a logical sequence piece, where the next paragraph answers a question that most readers will find themselves asking naturally, as they read the previous paragraph. Here's the same text, but with the questions deleted:

Most of us appreciate that unhealthy food affects our physical health, but sometimes we forget that a writer's most important body part, our brain, is part of that same physical body. It's where our creativity occurs and it is the third largest organ in our body, so feeding it with the right food will make it fitter, healthier, productive and more positive.

If you're settling down to add another 5,000 words to the novel, then you need a good breakfast: one that will provide you with stamina and sustenance for several hours. This is the most important meal of the day. When the University of Bristol undertook a study of 126 volunteers, aged between 20 and 79 years old, and assessed their mental health, it was those who ate breakfast everyday who were less depressed, less stressed and had lower perceived levels of stress than those who missed breakfast.

A good brain-enhancing breakfast should include wholegrain to provide carbohydrates that slowly release energy throughout the morning. Skipping breakfast encourages stressed writers to grab sugary snacks, containing ineffective simple carbohydrates. Whilst they provide a quick energy boost, it's short-lived, unsustainable and ultimately demoralising.

As the morning wears on, our creative productivity drops. If you're interviewing people for those all-important quotes, your brain needs to be alert to ensure you ask all the right questions. Give yourself a banana boost. Bananas contain three natural sugars: sucrose, fructose and glucose. These provide a quick energy boost and sustained energy uplift too. In addition to healthy fibre, bananas contain tryptophan, an amino acid needed by the body to produce the mood-enhancing hormone, serotonin. When released, serotonin gives a relaxing, contented feeling, relieving emotional tension. Bananas are also packed with vitamin C, B6, potassium, magnesium and folate. Researchers in India also discovered that people who ate two bananas a day for a week successfully lowered their blood pressure by 10%.

See? It still makes sense without the questions. So even though it isn't an interview piece, we've used the Q&A structure to give the article a logical sequence structure, where each paragraph expands upon a new point.

When you analyse your target publication you may come across other structures, but these I've identified here are the most common. Give your article a structure to hang your idea on and you'll find writing the bulk of your piece much easier. That just leaves the small problem of knowing how to begin and end your article. Now we've written the middle, it's time to go back and take a look at the beginning…

Chapter Five

Beginnings

Beginnings can be troublesome. They're even more troublesome if you haven't produced an outline. I understand the desire, once you've had an idea, to start writing. There's an urge to get it down on paper, before you forget it. Well, you can still do that with an outline. But, when you sit down, with no real plan about what exactly you're going to say, or whom you're saying it to, it can take a while to get things sorted out in your head. In the meantime, you've probably written three or four paragraphs, and it's only at this point, when everything has gone 'ping' in your mind, that you know where you're going.

The problem is, in this situation, those first three paragraphs need to be cut. In reality, when you've reached the point where you've clarified in your mind what exactly it is you want to say, that's where your real beginning is. Many first draft articles can be improved by cutting the first two or three paragraphs. Try it sometime.

However, if you're following this book you will hopefully find beginnings become a little easier. With an outline you know what it is you're going to say. With your market analysis you know whom you're saying it to. And if you've identified your article structure, you may already have written the middle section of your article. As I said earlier, just because an article has a beginning, a middle and an end, you don't have to write it in that order. If you know what you've said in your middle then writing the beginning becomes easier because you have a clear idea of what your beginning needs to introduce the reader to.

Beginnings have several important jobs to do:

- Sometimes they have to help explain a quirky title.
- They MUST engage an editor's interest - enough to make them want to read the rest of the article.
- Which means they MUST also engage a reader's interest. (It can be useful imagining that you're writing for the most bored readers on the planet. How would you engage their interest?)
- It needs to explain what the article is going to be about. (Which is why it can be useful to write the main part of the article first - because then you know what it's about.) It needs to tell the reader what it's going to tell them. By the end of the first paragraph the reader should know what your article is going to discuss, or the angle you're going to take. They will then make a judgment about whether to read on. The beginning is your sales pitch to the reader.

There are several ways you can start your articles, and again, you may spot a style, or trend during your market analysis.

A Great, Or Startling, Statement

Hit the reader with a startling fact or statement, and immediately they will want to know more. It encourages them to read on.

It is said that shipping magnate Benjamin Flounders built his 18th century Shropshire hill-top folly so he could watch his ships coming into dock at Liverpool and Bristol from the same vantage point.

This is how I began a piece in *BBC Countryfile* magazine about a folly built on top of a hill by Benjamin Flounders. I wanted readers to ask themselves whether it really is possible to see these two ports from this vantage point. And how did

Benjamin Flounders know how high to build his folly? And what did he do on cloudy days?

The answers are revealed later on in the article. As the crow flies, the distance between Bristol and Liverpool docks is about 220km, so that's some distance. Even if both docks were visible from this viewpoint, it suggests Benjamin Flounders had blooming good eyesight. Of course, it's not possible to see both docks from the top of the folly, but it's the sort of statement that encourages a reader to find out more (and hopefully, go and visit the folly to find out what it is possible to see from the top. It's a stunning view in all directions.)

If it wasn't for a man born 200 years ago at Much Wenlock, in Shropshire, the London 2012 Olympic Games may not have taken place.

This was how I began an article about Dr William Penny Brookes, a GP, a Magistrate and a thoroughly decent chap, who worked out that if you educated people, and kept them healthy by giving them regular physical exercise, then they were more likely to prosper and less likely to get drunk and fall into crime. As well as creating the town's first library, he also established the Wenlock Olympic Games (which still run to this day) and became hugely influential in re-establishing the modern Olympic movement that we see today. As an intriguing fact it works well, because few people outside of Shropshire have heard of Dr Brookes, yet everyone knows about the modern Olympic Games and what a worldwide spectacle they've become. How could someone who came from a sleepy, rural market town in a county many people couldn't place on a map, have been so influential in a worldwide phenomenon?

That's what a great or startling statement does. It raises lots of questions in the readers' mind, and so they continue reading in order to find out the answers.

Dialogue Or Quotes

"Marry my husband. Or at least kidnap him."

The beauty of dialogue is that the reader feels that person is talking directly to them. This makes it harder to ignore, because, generally speaking, we pay attention when people talk to us. (I am aware that some men have an affliction called selective hearing, which means they don't always hear everything that is directed at them, and, indeed, I was diagnosed with this affliction aged four.) But, usually, dialogue succeeds in drawing readers into an article.

In this example, from an article of mine in *Freelance Market News*, the dialogue is also a startling statement, so you can see we're combining two forms of beginnings here, and that can be a great way to strengthen an opening. If you've interviewed someone for your article, and you're using a selection of quotes throughout the piece to add credence and authority to your text, check out your quotes to see if you have something that would make a great opening. Giving your expert the first word also tells your readership that you've sourced experts in the topic you're discussing.

Here's another example, from a piece I had in a walking magazine:

"Solvitur Ambulando," he shouted, as he dashed past me on the path to Watergate Farm, near Loweswater.

Now, I don't know how good your Latin is, but if it's anything like mine then this phrase will mean nothing to you. Sometimes, a strange or unusual, piece of dialogue can work well, because it confuses. It gets the reader asking questions again. *What does this mean? What was the man talking about?* And so the reader continues in their quest to find out.

It's something else to bear in mind for travel articles. Quote a short snippet of dialogue in a foreign language in your opening and you're helping to set the scene.

Another reason dialogue intrigues readers is because we're nosey. We love eavesdropping, and some of the best pieces of dialogue come from when writers eavesdrop, or borrow other people's comments. I used a snippet of an overheard conversation to open an article I'd written about the Mortimer Trail footpath. I went into a card shop, to buy a postcard of Ludlow, where the trail starts, and as I stepped in through the door, the manageress was just coming out of the stock room and shouted across the shop floor to her assistant at the till: "*We need more kangaroos!*" It certainly grabbed the editor's attention, who went on to buy the article.

Scene Setting

The previous two examples have been about grabbing the reader's attention and dragging them into your article. Not all beginnings need to have such a violent, or forceful, manner. Some publications like a gentler style, where the reader is calmly lulled into a relaxed state for the piece they've sat down to read with a cup of coffee. These beginnings often work well for longer articles, where there is time to paint a picture and set the scene. They're often used to set the mood and tone of the article.

A January mist swirls across the surface of the water, swallowing all that rises from its depths. The still, cold air is broken by the frantic call of a startled tufted duck and the occasional 'plop' is accompanied by a tiny ripple that floats towards us. Standing at the end of the jetty, our eyes try to penetrate the moisture molecules the wintry sun hasn't yet gained the strength to evaporate. Llangorse Lake, it seems, wants to hold onto its secrets a little longer.

This introduction comes from a piece used during a six-year column I had in a local magazine called *Country & Border Life*. Notice how I've drawn upon several of my senses to help set the scene here. I've told readers what I could feel (the air is cold), hear (the frantic calls of the tufted duck and the occasional 'plop' of a jumping fish), as well as what I could see. And don't forget your sense of smell and taste, if it's appropriate for your setting.

It's a gentler-paced opening: one where the reader can think about what they've read.

An Anecdote

The right anecdote can help introduce a theme, or strand, to your article. Think of an anecdote as a little scene, or event, that helps the reader to place the context of the article. Here's an example from a feature of mine about Shropshire's Long Mynd, in *Country Walking* magazine:

"Earthquake!" shouts a young lad to his geology classmates. Playing for laughs, he falls off a small rock and collapses into fits of laughter. His friends join in with their own mock-tremors, but soon get back to their lesson, standing beside the crisp, cool waters of the stream. As classrooms go, Carding Mill Valley, with its rugged hills and beautiful beck, beats any I was ever schooled in.

Note the dialogue used right at the start. I hope you can picture the scene here, of school children playing in the stream, while they're supposed to be learning about geology. The reason I used this anecdote is because my article focused on the Long Mynd's geology and how it came to be where it is, and the fact that the surrounding geology does suffer from the occasional earth tremor. The earthquake dialogue, whilst at first seeming like kids mucking about, will actually become clearer as the reader continues with the article.

Ask A Question

Depending upon the subject matter, one way to grab the reader's interest is to ask them a direct question, which, hopefully, they won't know the answer to, so they'll read on to find out.

What's the first thing you do in the morning? Get dressed? Make a cup of tea? Artist Julia Cameron suggests that if you want to increase your creativity and writing productivity, you should pick up a notebook and start writing … three pages.

This was how I opened an article in *Writers' Forum* magazine about how to improve your creativity. Asking a direct question forces the reader to consider their response. When they've thought about it, they'll then read on to find out whether they were right or wrong, or whether they should have thought about something else. In this opening paragraph I have answered the question with what I'm going to be talking about - Julia Cameron's Morning Pages technique. (It's a useful technique. If you want to know more, check out her book: The Artist's Way, published by Pan, ISBN: 978-0330343589.)

But although I've answered my question, I haven't answered it fully. The reader doesn't actually know what they're supposed to be writing about, first thing in the morning. Nor do they know whether they can or can't write about specific things. Nor do they know if it has to be creative writing, or simply a to do list. The opening still raises some questions that need answering … and so they read on.

You don't have to ask a direct question of the reader. You can still begin a piece by asking a question that you don't need the reader to answer:

Will it? Or won't it? Every time there's a frisson of excitement as I twist the metal door handle and push.

This is how I started a piece for an article in *The Simple Things* about unlocked churches. Whenever I'm out walking and pass a church I always try the door, simply because these are interesting buildings and you never know what you may find inside. (Top tip: you can find some great article ideas in churches - like the memorial plaque in an Eardisley church that reads like the plot of Charles Dickens' *Bleak House* and guess what? Dickens is known to have visited that very church.) Sadly, many rural churches are locked these days and it's not always possible to step inside. So the opening of this article reflects the question I find myself asking as I'm about to turn the door handle. Will it, or won't it open?

The Topical Hook

I mentioned in the chapter about ideas that having a topical hook can give your idea more interest to an editor. If you're going down that route then it makes sense to tell the editor, and the reader, about this topical hook as soon as possible: i.e. at the beginning of your article.

'If February is the month of 'lurve' then Wales and its Borders is the loved up destination to head to. From passionate panoramas to loving landscapes, there's a romantic spot for everyone in the heart of this region for Valentine's Day.

This article is clearly targeted at the February issue.

When the Rev E Donald Carr failed to return after conducting a service at the neighbouring village church, 24 hours after setting out on 29th January 1865 in one of Shropshire's worst storms, his parishioners announced his death. Reverend Carr had other ideas.

It probably won't surprise you to learn that this article appeared in a January issue of a magazine *(BBC Countryfile)*. It's important that you make the topical connection in your article as early as possible, because it explains why your piece appears in this particular issue.

When you analyse your target publication, read all of the opening paragraphs of the articles, in particular the articles in the section or slot that you're targeting. If you spot a common style or theme, then it makes sense to use that style for your own idea. It all helps make your submission fit into the general tone of your target publication.

Writing beginnings needn't be the tricky challenge that some writers think it is. Once you know the style and tempo of the piece, and are clear with what it is your article is discussing, launching into the beginning should become much easier.

While we've looked at beginnings here, there are a couple of things that we need to think about, that come before our article beginnings …

Titles

There are two schools of thoughts when it comes to titles: just give your piece any straightforward title, because the editor will probably change it anyway, or put some effort into creating your title, because it's the first thing the editor sees.

I'm going to put forward a third school of thought: do what you see in your market analysis. (Go on, admit it. You're getting bored with this market analysis stuff now, aren't you?) I take the attitude that if you're trying to submit work to a particular publication then you need to adopt as many of its ways as possible - and that includes the titles. And, in the great scheme of things, flicking through the pages looking at the titles of all the main articles does not take much time, but it can be so revealing. Here's a selection of titles from *Family Traveller* magazine:

- Scandi Crush (holidaying in Scandinavia)
- Summer Daze (cool cloths for kids to wear)
- The Tan Commandments (how to stay safe in the sun)
- Pitch perfect (ten great places to go camping in Europe)

Are you spotting a trend here? This magazine appears to like a play on words for their titles. So if I were going to target them with an idea, I would try to give my article a title that was also a play on words.

Here is a selection of titles from *Waterways World*:

- The Oxford Canal in 1954
- Venice By Boat
- Making A Shelving Unit
- Buying A New Boat?
- Exploring Ashby

Now these titles do exactly what they say on the tin. Notice how I didn't have to explain them in parentheses, like I did with the *Family Traveller* titles. These titles don't need any explanation, because they describe what the articles are about.

Another title style to look out for includes alliteration, where the first letter of each word is the same: *Seven Stupendous Slimming Secrets*.

It doesn't take long to determine what a particular magazine's title style is, but I think it's worth taking a couple of minutes to check that your title fits in. It's something else that indicates to the editor that you've looked at their magazine and know what their readers like.

Standfirsts

Occasionally, you may come across a piece of text that comes between the title and the opening paragraph of an article. It's called a standfirst, and is often no more than 20 or 30 words that tell the reader what the article is about. It usually includes the writer's byline or credit too, but not always. Again, (you know what I'm going to say here, don't you?) take a look through your target market to see if they use them. Not every magazine does.

Here's the standfirst for the first article in my column in *Writing Magazine*:

Launching a new series on managing the business side of your writing, freelance Simon Whaley helps you start the new tax year on the right foot by getting your finances in order.

Here's another from the series:

Reliable records of contacts, submissions, contracts and commissions are essential to keep your writing business organised and financially sound, says Simon Whaley.

And my folly piece in *BBC Countryfile* began with:

A stroll through the Shropshire countryside reveals a historic folly with epic views across the Welsh Marches.

Country Walking magazine rewrote my standfirst suggestion, which I supplied when they commissioned me to write an article about the Long Mynd. They went for:

Discover big views, tranquil hollows, ancient rocks, wild horses and avian choirs on the slopes of England's long mountain …

A standfirst usually appears in a larger font size than your main article, but a smaller one than the font size used for your title, so it's designed to stand out and grab the reader's attention. I often find they work in combination with the title. For example, my *Country Walking* title was *Skylarks and Seismic Shifts*, which doesn't tell the reader a lot about where the article is about, although when they read they piece they'll understand the meaning of the title. So the standfirst goes a little way into explaining to the reader what the article is about.

Don't get me wrong: if you don't produce a standfirst and the magazine uses them, the editor isn't going to reject your piece because you haven't done a complete job. There are some editors who prefer to write all of the standfirsts, rewriting those that the writers have submitted. Well, that's fine. At the end of the day, the editor is the boss, so they can do what they like. Sometimes my standfirsts get rewritten, sometimes they get used exactly as I write them. I just feel that as a supplier, I should give the customer everything they need. If I see the magazine uses standfirsts I provide one. If they don't, then I don't either. It's as simple as that.

Now that we've got the beginnings sorted, it's now time to look at what to do in the end …

Chapter Six

Endings

Endings are just as important as beginnings, if not more so. A reader has given up some of their time to read your words, so it's only right that you bring your piece to a natural conclusion. Don't stop suddenly, because readers will feel cheated, as if they're missing half of the action. Indeed, I was on Facebook recently (networking, of course) and somebody commented that a short story had finished awkwardly, and she didn't feel all the loose ends had been tied up. Suddenly, several other readers piled into the conversation, agreeing, and thankful that it wasn't just them who thought it had ended abruptly. Many of them agreed to contact the magazine. That's what can happen when readers feel they're missing out.

So by carefully constructing a satisfying ending to your article you can keep your readers happy. Endings should:

- Make the reader feel that the writer has achieved what the opening set out to do. (If you've just written your beginning, then it's still clear in your mind what you've told the reader your article will set out to achieve.)
- Be fulfilling and satisfying.
- Attempt to end on a positive note.

Just like beginnings, there are several ways in which you can round off your articles, and some of the ways may seem familiar.

Summarising The Main Point

Sometimes your conclusion simply needs to summarise the main points of your article again. There's a suggested structure for giving talks and presentations to a group of people:

- tell them what you're going to talk to them about (introduction),
- tell them what you want to tell them (main body),
- then tell them what you've told them (ending).

A summary paragraph follows this format, concisely reminding readers what they've been told. Here are a couple of examples:

This one is from *Country & Border Life* magazine:

As you can see, Welsh coastal castles are some of the best to be found anywhere in the UK. They were built to withstand attacks and, as such, have stood the test of time too. Of course, getting inside them today is a little easier, and a far more enjoyable experience.

And here's one from an article I wrote about why writers should have a last will and testament, which was published in *Writing Magazine:*

Nobody wants to think about their death, but we're in a fortunate position where our words become a piece of intellectual property that we can leave for future generations to enjoy and exploit. Don't give relations extra grief or heartache at a difficult time by not leaving clear instructions for what should happen to your creations. The cost of this piece of mind could be easily covered by the sale of an article or short story.

Circular Structure

A circular ending refers back to a point you made in your opening paragraph. This has the effect of returning your reader to where you first captured their imagination. This can work particularly well with a journey structure for the main section of your article. I also think it emphasizes the journey the reader's mind has been on. There they were, flicking through the magazine, when your opening grabbed their attention and pulled them into your article, which they've now read and reached the end. By commenting on something you mentioned at the beginning you're returning them to the point where you dragged them in, as if you're saying, "*Okay, you can carry on flicking through the magazine again now.*" (I know, I'm mad, but I like to think my articles have taken readers away from reality momentarily, and now, with a circular ending, I'm gently dropping them back into the present.)

To fully appreciate the circular structure, it's necessary to remind ourselves of some article openings. Here's the opening and closing sentences for my Unlocked Churches piece in *The Simple Things*:

Opening: *Will it? Or won't it? Every time there's a frisson of excitement as I twist the metal door handle and push.*

Closing: *Nothing beats that sense of anticipation as our fingers curl around the door handle and twist. Will it? Or won't it?*

Here, the final closing words are the same as the opening words of the article. But not only that, there's also a reference to the emotion. The opening tells the reader of the frisson of excitement, and the ending reminds them of that with the anticipation.

Do you remember my anecdotal opening for my article in *Country Walking* magazine?

"Earthquake!" shouts a young lad to his geology classmates. Playing for laughs, he falls off a small rock and collapses into fits of laughter. His friends join in with their own mock-tremors, but soon get back to their lesson, standing beside the crisp, cool waters of the stream. As classrooms go, Carding Mill Valley, with its rugged hills and beautiful beck, beats any I was ever schooled in.

Here's how I ended it:

At the National Trust's Chalet Pavilion, the geology students pack up for the day. Thankfully, there were no seismic shifts to disrupt their studies today. In fact, underfoot, the Long Mynd feels pretty solid. I sense it'll be hanging around here a little while longer yet.

The circular structure here brings the reader back to those geology students I threw their attention on at the start of the piece. But there's also a nod to the earthquake comment too, when I mention about everything underfoot still feeling pretty solid.

Try to make your circular endings feel natural. If you force them they don't feel as satisfying. If you have to alter the flow of your text, or the style you're writing in to achieve the circular reference, then look for a different ending. There are still several types to choose from.

A Call To Arms

This is where you encourage your reader to get off their bottoms and do something now. In theory, your article has given them all the information they need to do or create something, so all that's left is for them to get out of their chair, go off and do it.

Here's the ending to my article about Julia Cameron's Morning Pages technique:

If you're looking to keep your brain in gear, Morning Pages could be the way to start your day. What are you waiting for?

And this is how I rounded off a travel feature about the Royal Yacht Britannia in *Scotland magazine:*

The next time you're in Edinburgh, step aboard the Royal Yacht Britannia and discover its magic for yourself.

This form of ending is generally positive and upbeat. Your article has empowered the reader with this knowledge, which means they have no excuse not to go and do it.

Dialogue And Quotes

If you've interviewed somebody, and used one of their quotes to open your piece, then giving them the last word can also be a nice way to round things off. Choose a phrase that either encapsulates the whole article idea, neatly rounds off your topic on an upbeat note, or offers further expert advice.

Here's the ending to an article in *Country Walking* magazine that I wrote about hot air ballooning:

It was a wonderful experience. Helen stands back from the basket, raises her glass of champagne high in the air and says, "That was heaven!"

A quote can also be a useful way of adding some balance to an article. For *Country & Border Life* magazine I'd interviewed an expert about foraging for wild food on beaches and, overall, my article was a positive piece showing people that all of this free food existed. But it was also important to remind readers that we are not the only animal species who might rely on this food supply, and the best way of doing this was to give my expert the final say:

"Foraging with respect, common sense and self-restraint is the best way," says Fergus. "It's important not to view all wild food purely in terms of their potential as human food. Learning about the other species that form a web of dependency upon all of these items is important, because we need

to understand that what we take is then not there for other species who need it more. That's why we should only take a little of what we find, and leave the rest for the other creatures to feed upon. Understanding the whole food chain is such a fascinating subject in itself."

You could argue that giving the last word to the same person that you gave the first word to, is also an example of a circular structure.

Looking Forward

There may be times when you write an article on a difficult or challenging subject, but find that working out how to end it is problematic, especially if you're looking for an upbeat resolution. One possible way is to look forward to the future.

I wrote an article for *Writing Magazine* that discussed the topic of whether writers can be carers. When family members are ill our need to be alone to write can find itself in conflict with our duty of looking after a loved one. Finding that balance between the two can be troublesome, and it is easy for despondency to set in. With some illnesses there will only be one way they can end so I was having trouble working out how to bring it to a conclusion. I'd interviewed an expert from Carers UK, and I'd been planning on using a quote to round off the piece, but for me, the best quote didn't end on as positive a note as I wanted. In the end, my solution was to look to the future:

None of us knows what lies around the corner of life. When a family crisis arises, family comes first, but remember that you are part of that family too. So don't stop writing. Acknowledge that life will be stressful, but learn to adapt. Adjust your goals, and find ways to continue with your writing projects. "Getting support is good not just for the carers but for their loved ones they support too," reminds Steve. Remember that thought, because no matter what is round the next corner, your writing can give you the strength that you need to offer them that support.

I was surprised by the response from readers this article generated. For several months afterwards, the magazine's letters page had numerous letters thanking me for writing it. It seems there are many writers out there who care for others, and several of them were beating themselves up over the conflict they were having between spending time looking after their loved ones and spending time on their own writing. I hope my final sentence told them that it was important for them to be selfish in the future, because it's this that would give them the strength to carry on.

Another article looked at techniques dog owners could use to desensitise their dogs to the frightening noise and sudden bangs that fireworks make. I ended this by saying:

In multicultural Britain, fireworks are an all-year round annoyance to owners with nervous dogs. But by following the tips shown here, firework displays in the future should be less stressful for you and your faithful friend.

Again, it ends by offering hope and suggesting that life in the future can be better.

Now, what with our middles, beginnings and endings sorted, you might think that that's the end of our article-writing process. Sorry! There are still a few more things to consider, I'm afraid …

Chapter Seven

Other Page Furniture

Rarely, these days, will you see just an article of text on a page. Usually, there is a plethora of other material accompanying it: boxouts, side panels, photographs, further information boxes, or pull quotes (where a piece of text on the page is used at a larger font size). This is sometimes known as *page furniture*. It is used to break up a page and designed to make it more interesting to the eye. Readers often glance at this information first to see if they want to commit to reading the full article.

An important point to consider is that it is not your job to decide where on the page all of this information goes; that is down to the magazine's own designers. However, you do need to provide the text that makes up these extra sections of information. (The only exception are pull quotes - the magazine's staff decide which words or phrases they want to emphasize, if they use this feature.)

Although this information will form part of your overall article, think of it as additional information. If the editor decided not to use any page furniture, your article should still work on its own, without any of this additional material. I like to think of this as the bonus material on a DVD.

Boxouts, Side Panels And Further Information Sections

All this extra information comes with a variety of names, but, essentially, they all come down to the same thing: a separate section offering additional information that complements your article's text. Often it appears within a box, or a shaded section, but you don't have to worry about that. All you're concerned with is the text.

Here are some common uses for such sections:

- Travel articles almost always have these sections, designed to give the reader enough information so they can follow in the writer's footsteps. Who flies there? What currency is used? What are the opening times and entry fees? It is common for travel articles in one magazine to have further information boxes that follow the same format. For example, *BBC Countryfile's* Great Days Out Section always has a further information section giving readers information about where to stay, where to eat and what else to do in the area. When you go through and do your market analysis look out for these panels and see if they all follow the same format. If they do then you know that you need to provide the same information too.
- Do you need to explain key words? If your market analysis suggests that not all of the readership will understand acronyms and abbreviations then a glossary of terms could work well as a separate boxout.
- Do you have information that complements your article? An article about the health benefits of a particular food might warrant a recipe using that food product. The recipe could be used in a separate box.
- A case study is often used as a boxout. It's not part of your main article, but it adds to the message of your main article.
- Contacts and Further Information - articles that offer readers information usually only scratch the surface. If piqued, readers may want more, so a list of useful website and postal addresses might be beneficial. A health article may offer website addresses of charities

and support groups. These days practically every organisation and society has a website address. If there are too many to include within the main body of your article, collecting them all together into a *Where To Find Further Information* panel can work better.

- Interesting facts about your topic can often be collated into a boxout. It's so tempting to want to include everything you've discovered in your research in your article, but that may not be possible. Sometimes you may find bullet-pointing a series of quirky or interest facts makes a great additional boxout section.
- Reviews (eg, restaurant reviews) might have two lists: What We Liked and What We Didn't Like. Often, full contact details are given. (If you've reviewed a restaurant readers like it if you give them the full address and phone number so they can book a table themselves, and know where to go.) Do such reviews use a grading system? If so, this information may appear as a boxout.

The more you look at articles the more often you will see these additional sections of information. When it comes to presenting your work, I've already said don't put all of this information inside a text box, or coloured background. The magazine's production staff will only have to take it out again. All you need to do is give them the text. The simplest way to do this is at the end of your article. Give your further information section a heading. (If you're following a template that you've spotted in your target publication then use the same headings the magazine uses.) Then, underneath this heading, provide the information.

Sometimes I offer editors a range of further information panels, which allows them to pick and choose what they want to use. They don't always use them all. When I submit articles, I send two word counts - the article word count and then a word count for the additional boxouts.

Boxout Tips

- Keep them short and sweet. Bullet-points are great for boxouts.
- Never put them inside a box. When writing your text, at the end of your article just give your boxout a title and then put the information underneath. Don't use a different font, don't put it inside a text box, and don't use different coloured text. Keep things plain and simple.
- Copy what you see in your target publication. If you spot that all boxouts in your target publication follow a set format, make sure yours does the same.

(These bullet points would make an ideal boxout section.)

Contributor Biography And Photo

While we're still talking about additional information to accompany your article, it's worth taking a moment to consider what information is required about you: the writer. There's an increasing trend for magazines to give readers a snippet of information about this month's contributors. Sometimes this information appears as a panel near the contents page (which is great, because it's an excellent indicator that the magazine uses freelance material). Alternatively, a magazine may use some biographical information at the end of the article you've written.

If you spot this when you undertake your market analysis it's worth considering putting something together to include with your submission.

From a practical point of view, I place my biography at the end of my article (and after any boxouts), and give it the heading: *biography*. (Earth-shattering, I know, but at least it does what it says on the tin.)

So, what do you tell readers about yourself? That you managed to swim 25 metres the wrong way in the swimming pool aged seven, in your pyjamas, and still get your swimming proficiency certificate? It may be applicable if your article is about swimming, but readers want to know what's relevant. The golden rule, which I hope is coming across in this book now, is to follow the examples you see in your target publication.

I have a couple of biographies I use (they're all about me, I hasten to add), which I select, depending upon the type of publication. I tailor my biography to the subject matter and readership. If you think back to the chapter about ideas I mentioned that it's possible to sell an idea to an editor because you're selling your experience. Your biography needs to reflect this, because this is what sells you as the expert to the readership too.

Here's my biography for a general walking publication:

Simon Whaley lives in the South Shropshire Area of Outstanding Natural Beauty and explores it on foot every day. He's written for numerous walking publications and is the author of Best Walks in the Welsh Borders, and the humorous Bluffers Guide to Hiking.

I sometimes write for Lakeland Walker magazine, which focuses on walking in the English Lake District. So my general walking biography isn't quite right for them, and a little adaptation is required.

Simon Whaley is a regular visitor to the Lake District. He's particularly adept at timing his visits to coincide with torrential rain.

When I wrote the article about techniques for calming your dog during periods of fireworks, I had to tailor my biography towards that particular readership, like so:

Simon Whaley is a Shropshire-based freelance writer and the bestselling author of One Hundred Ways For A Dog To Train Its Human *(written when his Golden Retriever had finished training him).*

Note how most magazines are not looking for something to give a celebrity memoir a run for their money. Instead they need something short and sweet: a couple of sentences, if that. It's worth spending some time creating a batch of different biographies for the different markets you want to write for. Not only does it mean you'll have them to hand when you need them, but it's also a good exercise at identifying your areas of expertise. It's a great place to mention books, obviously, but don't think you need to have written a book. You don't. Concentrate on your area of expertise. For the piece in *Country Walking* magazine about hot air ballooning, the biography I submitted was as follows:

Simon Whaley has taken to the skies twice in a hot air balloon: first from the sedate shire of Surrey and later from the rural hinterland of Shropshire. He now knows the difference between a drop line and a crown line.

It's enough to demonstrate that I have experience of hot air ballooning, and know what I'm talking about.

In addition to the biography, you'll also see a photo. Now, I know this scares the oojamaflips out of some people, but let's put things into perspective here. (I hate having my photo take too.) If you look at the photos, most are thumbnail sized, if not smaller. Most are simply looking for a head and shoulders shot, of you looking calm and relaxed.

Avoid cropping a photo you already have, taken on holiday eight years ago, when you got completely bladdered and don't remember who took it. The chances are, you won't be looking at your best and there'll be some lamppost, speed restriction sign or tree growing out of your head. There may even be someone else's arm draped around your neck, but who it belongs to nobody knows because of the way you've cropped the photo. Instead, get a friend to take a head and shoulders photo of you, standing against a plain background, using an ordinary compact camera.

Like biographies, it can be useful to have more than

one contributor photo. I have a standard head and shoulders image, but I also have one of me out in the hills, used for walking and outdoor magazines, some of me sitting at my computer (for the writing magazines) and even photos of me giving workshops and talks (used with the photographer's permission).

If you can, ensure your contributor photo reflects the subject matter you're writing about. If you write about gardening topics then your photo should show you in a garden (not necessarily your own, although that would be better), and those who write about cars invariably pose through the driver's window of the flashiest car they've ever test-driven. *Outdoor Photography* places its contributor biographies and images together near the contents page at the start of the magazine. There are twelve in total, and in one issue four photos have the contributors holding a camera, while eleven show them outdoors.

At the end of the day, any contributor photo is better than none. You're not going to have your piece about life on the International Space Station rejected because your contributor photo doesn't show you in space, or on the station. But if you can, it's worth supplying an appropriate photo, because this is what the reader will use to judge you as an expert on the subject you're writing about.

Chapter Eight

Adding Creativity To Your Non-Fiction

Creative non-fiction? This probably sounds like an oxymoron. Surely the whole point about non-fiction is that it relates to facts, not fiction. So how can you be creative with facts? Well, you're not being creative with the facts but with *how you convey* those facts.

I mention creative non-fiction here because there are a series of techniques you can use to add more spice to your articles. As I commented near the start of this book, our articles should entertain as well as inform, and creative non-fiction is one way of inserting some entertainment into your article.

American journalists began experimenting in the 1960s, at a time when newspapers were introducing colour supplements in the weekend editions, and these were looking for different types of features. One American writer, Tom Wolfe, wrote a piece for *Esquire* magazine about the Hot Rod and Custom Car culture of Southern California. Entitled *There Goes (Varoom! Varoom!) That Kandy-Kolored Tangerine-Flake Streamline Baby*, it caused a stir when it hit the newsstands. Loved by some and hated by others (because it was so different), Wolfe demonstrated that it was possible to report non-fiction facts in an engaging and entertaining way. (Incidentally, Wolfe published this and many others of his articles in a collection of the same title, which is still available today, and you might find it interesting reading.)

One of Wolfe's opening sentences mentions the word *hernia* 57 times. You can't get much more different than that from a typical journalistic opening sentence. He used this to describe the sound of a large room full of hundreds of people having hundreds of different conversations. He couldn't make out what was being said. All he could hear was a general hubbub of chatting, and the best way he could find of describing what he heard was as if everyone was saying the word *hernia.* (If you can persuade a group of friends - and it's probably best if they're close friends - to say *hernia* over and over again, you'll find that it works well. It does sound like the background noise of people chatting.)

This new form of writing was first called New Journalism, but has also been called Narrative Non-Fiction, The Art of Fact, The Art of Non-Fiction, Reality Fiction, and Literary Non-Fiction, although today it is more commonly known as Creative Non-Fiction. There are four key creative non-fiction techniques that writers of travel, biography, food, nature and personal experience (to name a few) can use to add further interest to their articles. They are:

Scene-By-Scene Construction

Instead of encapsulating the entire story in the first sentence, this techniques tells a story in a dramatic way, by grabbing the reader's attention with a powerful scene, and then using the technique of flashback to set that excitement into context. If it works for short story writers and novelists then why not article writers too?

Using Conversational Speech

Journalists use quotes. Creative non-fiction uses dialogue. There's a difference. Instead of reporting what was said, creative non-fiction uses dialogue in the same way it would be used in a short story or novel.

Point Of View

When a journalist writes about a news event they report the facts. They gather information from many sources to provide an impartial overview of what happened. In creative non-fiction, it's accepted that you can take the viewpoint of one person (which could be the writer's viewpoint) and describe their experience. Some creative non-fiction writers use their journalistic skills of interviewing people, to get an understanding of what an experience felt like, and then they write up the experience from that person's point of view, as if they were that person. (Ghost writers do something similar.) The key difference here is that journalists report what other people saw, whereas creative non-fiction writers write it as if they witnessed it.

The Writer Can Be A Primary Source

Journalists are taught to use primary sources. They must source their information from the right person, not from someone who heard via the cat's mother. However, creative non-fiction appreciates that the writer can be a primary source of information too. They can be eye-witnesses as well. By making the writer a primary source of information, they put themselves into the story. Journalists don't do this with news stories. Read any news story (or listen to the news on TV or the radio) and you won't know what the journalist thinks of the situation, because all they are doing is reporting the facts. They are trained to report information as impartially as possible, which is why they keep themselves out of the news stories. (You won't see the personal pronoun *I* in a news story.)

However, this creative non-fiction technique has infiltrated some areas of journalism today, particularly war correspondents. These journalists can't always access reliable, impartial information in a war zone, so they have to rely upon what they have witnessed. During times of war, security measures often prevent journalists from reporting the detailed information that they would like. But creative non-fiction allows them *convey the truth, without distorting the facts.*

Probably the most well-known example, was that of BBC news correspondent Brian Hanrahan, reporting from an aircraft carrier during the Falklands War. Unable to state the exact numbers of planes involved in a raid, he drew upon his own eyewitness account, using himself as a primary source, and said, "I counted them all out - and I counted them all back." So despite being unable to tell viewers how many planes were involved, he was still able to convey the truth that none of them was shot down, or lost in battle.

So let's look at each of these techniques in a little more detail …

Writing In Scenes

The Oxford English Dictionary describes as scene as: *a subdivision, or a unit, of drama.* In fiction, a scene usually happens in one location, or a moment of time, and that can work for non-fiction too.

Thinking about scenes can help in the planning stage of your article, particularly if you're going to use a chronological structure, or that of a journey. Thinking about each key point that you want to make as a distinct scene can prove useful.

Here's an article of mine, written as a series of scenes, that appeared in a walking magazine. It was used in a section of the magazine where writers analysed why they enjoyed walking, and what it is that draws walkers out into the open air. (Anyone would think I'd analysed the publication and targeted this piece at a specific section, eh?).

"Solvitur Ambulando," he shouted, as he dashed past me on the path to Watergate Farm, at Loweswater.

"Morning," I replied, wondering what the heck the at-least-80-year-old hiker was going on about as he made his way back towards Maggie's Bridge. Had he heard me muttering as I ambled towards the trees at Holme Wood? Probably. I know I have a habit of talking to myself when I'm out walking, but talking to yourself can be some of the best conversations a person can have. Sometimes I just get carried away and forget to whisper. And if a route suddenly gets busy, I have been known to hold a mobile phone to my ear, because people seem to find this more acceptable. That was until someone pointed out there was no mobile phone signal in the area I was walking.

I know I was having one of my more in-depth discussions with myself, because I was trying to resolve a problem. I'd been working for a particular client for some time and was getting frustrated at the amount of effort I was putting in for the meagre reward. Being self-employed, it's easy to say yes to any work that comes your way, because any work is better than no work, especially in this current economic climate. But that work/life balance equation rears its ugly head every so often, especially that phrase 'working to live, not living to work'.

Today was one of those days in the Lakes when you had to get outside. I frequently escape to the Lake District, but being self-employed, I often find myself doing some work whilst supposedly 'on holiday' – with so many self-catering properties and hotels having free Wi-Fi, these days, it's difficult to break free. And despite my earlier comment, I did once check my emails half way up the Old Man of Coniston. But today was one of those classic clear blue-sky days, with not enough moisture to make a wisp of cloud, and no wind to turn a leaf, let alone a wind turbine.

Normally, for me, it would have been a day to go high. I'm not one to set out to climb a mountain if it's guaranteed to be in cloud. If I've put effort in to ascend a summit I want to be rewarded with a view, or at least a sneaky peek of a view, and so days like this always have 'Go high!' stamped firmly across them. But as I contemplated where to go, my dilemma influenced my decision. If I went high, I'd be doing it because that what I always did. It's like saying 'yes' when someone offers me work. It's what I felt I ought to be doing. So, going against the grain, I decided to stay low. I wouldn't climb: I would circumnavigate instead. Which is why I found myself approaching the shores of Loweswater.

Stepping into Holme Wood, just where the National Trust moor their rowing boats, my mood changed. The only breeze was an air of tranquillity. It was the slightest of ripples that took the sharpness off the reflections in the water. A chiff-chaff sang its tuneful two-note song and a red squirrel teased me with a sighting before scampering behind the tree trunk.

As I followed the path around the edge of Loweswater, the trees hid the view. Only the dappled sunlight reached the woodland floor, and whereas normally, on a day like this, I'd be scanning huge vistas across half of northern England, and possibly a bit of Scotland, all I could see now were rays of sunshine spotlighting the individual veins on the beech leaves.

At Holme Wood Bothy I sat down and watched a fish wallowing in the warmth of the shallows. Ahead of me, I was seeing double: two Whitesides, two Grasmoors and two Mellbreaks. I sat there for twenty minutes drinking in the view, marvelling at the sight I was seeing, purely because I'd taken the unusual decision of staying low. "Life is more interesting when you do something different," I said out loud. Only the red squirrels heard me this time, and they didn't answer me back. So I did. "Perhaps that's the answer you're looking for."

My circumnavigation of contemplation continued around Loweswater, and after Hudson Place, I cut across the soggy fields and two footbridges to find the shore-side road, with its small layby. There, sitting in a chair with a newspaper and pipe, sat the gentleman who'd passed me earlier.

"Did you enjoy your walk?" I enquired.

"Of course," he replied. " How can you not enjoy yourself when you're doing something you want to do?"

I gazed across the water towards Carling Knott. "And do you enjoy everything that you do?"

"If I have a choice in what I'm doing, then yes. The skill is understanding you have a choice most of the time. In the grand scheme of things, there is little in life that we have to do by law."

I thought about my dilemma, as I watched a buzzard soaring on a thermal overhead. Perhaps this chap had something.

"You're nearly there," he said, turning a page of his paper.

"Yes," I replied. "I parked at Maggie's Bridge car park. I'm just wandering back there now."

"It wasn't your car, I was talking about."

"Sorry?"

"Your decision," he clarified. "You're nearly there. Solvitur Ambulando." He tapped the side of his nose.

"What does that mean, Solvitur Ambulando?" I enquired.

"I'm sure you can find out." He brought the paper up close to his face. Our conversation was over.

Wandering back along the road, I soon realised I was smiling. Grinning almost. The old gentleman was right. I had made my decision. I was going to tell my client to look for another supplier. I didn't have to work for him. There was no law that said I had to. I had a choice. Like today's decision about walking low and admiring the fells from the valley, instead of climbing to the summit. I'd done something different from what I felt I ought to be doing. And it felt great.

Back at the cottage I switched on my computer. I didn't check my emails. Instead I Googled the phrase Solvitur Ambulando and then nodded in agreement. That chap was right. Perhaps if I'd been taught Latin at school I'd have understood its meaning: you can solve it by walking.

Suddenly, it became clear. That's why I talk to myself when out walking. I'm trying to solve my current dilemma. And the best solutions can always be found when out in the fells.

If nothing else, you've learned two things from this piece: what *Solvitur Ambulando* means, and that I talk to myself when I'm out walking. But let's analyse the article in a little more detail. I see six distinct scenes in this piece:

- Scene 1 - Where the old man and I first meet.
- Scene 2 - a flashback, where I explain a bit of background information, my dilemma, the always climbing high on good weather days, etc.
- Scene 3 - Stepping into Holme Wood, where I spend time appreciating the smaller details of life: the veins on beech leaves, the fish wallowing in the warm waters.
- Scene 4 - Bumping into the old man again, and our conversation.
- Scene 5 - returning back to my car, realising I'd made my decision.
- Scene 6 - back at my cottage Googling Solvitur Ambulando.

This piece draws upon two structures. Firstly, it is a journey. I'm travelling around Loweswater, in the Lake District, and it's a route readers can identify on the map and follow. The piece also has a chronological structure, because it follows the sequence of events in order, with the exception for scenes 1 and 2, which have been swapped. Scene 1 has action in it, which hopefully draws the reader in. It also raises some questions in the reader's head:

- What does Solvitur Ambulando mean?
- Who is the old man?
- Why am I talking to myself? (Actually, I don't think that one's ever been answered.)
- Will I solve my problem?
- How will I solve my problem?
- Will I discover what Solvitur Ambulando means?

Each scene has a key role to play in answering those questions.

The first scene sets up those questions in the reader's mind. Scenes two and three explain why I'm talking to myself and convey my dilemma to the reader. It also begins to show how I will solve my problem, because it shows the pleasure I'm getting from doing something different: appreciating the smaller things in life. My decision to stay low was the correct one to take.

Scene four shows the old man helping me make my decision, because he's drawing upon his own experience and wisdom. Here's a man who knows what he's talking about. The next scene reveals a change. I've made a decision. I've resolved my dilemma and I appreciate that the walk has helped me achieve this.

The final scene reveals the definition of solvitur ambulando, which I like to think rounds off the piece neatly, by taking readers back to the start of the article where the words were first uttered.

Writing in scenes can give your non-fiction a story-like quality. It enables you to play around with the structure a bit. Had I written this in a true chronological order (of waking up in the morning and wondering whether to go high or low) the opening wouldn't have been strong enough to hook the reader, in my opinion. They would have turned the page before they reached the scene where I bumped into the old man who started spouting Latin at me.

Scenes enable you to jump from one interesting point to another. For example, between scenes three and four of this piece there's a distance of over a mile, but I didn't recount my experience along this section of my walk. I'm not saying this section of the walk was boring. Scenically it was outstanding. But what I experienced along this section wasn't relevant to the reader or to the article. The next sentence: *My circumnavigation of contemplation continued around Loweswater, and after Hudson Place, I cut across the soggy fields and two footbridges to find the shore-side road, with its small layby,* is what links scenes three and four together. Writing in scenes helps you to cut out the unnecessary bits.

Fiction writers are more aware about writing in scenes, but it's something non-fiction writers should consider too. It won't work for every article, but if you're planning on using a journey or chronological structure this technique can make an impact.

Using Dialogue

Quotes can add authority to your text. Interview an expert and use their quoted opinions in your article and your text then has credibility.

For example, your observational comment in an article that you've never seen so much rain fall in such a short space of time is useful because it helps demonstrate how much water fell from the sky. However, quote a meteorological expert in your article as saying, "*two and a half inches of rain fell in the space of one hour, which is more than in the previous three months put together,*" and readers will accept this as a fact. That's why journalists use quotes in news stories, because they tell the readers what the experts think, not what the journalist thinks.

Dialogue is different. Dialogue follows the classic writing mantra of *show, don't tell.* You can use it to give the reader information, move your article along and also reveal something about the people in your article who are speaking. I also think that dialogue involves the reader more. It helps to make them feel that they're listening in on the conversation, and that they're involved in the action.

Consider the scene from the Solvitur Ambulando piece earlier:

"Did you enjoy your walk?" I enquired.

"Of course," he replied. " How can you not enjoy yourself when you're doing something you want to do?"

I gazed across the water towards Carling Knott. "And do you enjoy everything that you do?"

"If I have a choice in what I'm doing, then yes. The skill is understanding you have a choice most of the time. In the grand scheme of things, there is little in life that we have to do by law."

I thought about my dilemma, as I watched a buzzard soaring on a thermal overhead. Perhaps this chap had something.

"You're nearly there," he said, turning a page of his paper.

"Yes," I replied. "I parked at Maggie's Bridge car park. I'm just wandering back there now."

"It wasn't your car, I was talking about."

"Sorry?"

"Your decision," he clarified. "You're nearly there. Solvitur Ambulando." He tapped the side of his nose.

"What does that mean, Solvitur Ambulando?" I enquired.

"I'm sure you can find out." He brought the paper up close to his face. Our conversation was over.

The dialogue shows the elderly chap's understanding, both of my situation, and also of life. I like to think he comes across as a bit of a sage: someone with a wealth of wisdom gained from the experience of life. That wisdom is also conveyed through dialogue. He says, "*There is little in life that we have to do by law.*" That's the key piece of information that helps me reach my decision.

Written differently, I could have reported his words, like so: *An old man, sitting by the water's edge reading a newspaper, said, "There is little in life we have to do by law."*

However, because the speech has been *reported* the writer is telling the reader what was said. The reader is getting the information second-hand. Dialogue changes this. It gives the spoken words some immediacy, as if the reader is there, listening in as they are being spoken.

Revealing The Truth

I have a confession to make. I mentioned at the start of this chapter that creative non-fiction allows you to be artistic with how you convey the truth. Dialogue is one way of doing this. My trip around Loweswater is a true event. I was in a dilemma, deciding what step to take with a troublesome client of mine. And I did bump into the same old man twice on my walk: once near the start of my walk, and then again about half way round, where he was relaxing by the lake with his newspaper. However, those conversations did not happen. I made them up. The real conversations went something like this:

Conversation 1

"Morning."
"Morning."
"Glorious day."
"Isn't it just?"

Conversation 2

"Hello again."
"Hello."
"Relaxing after you run?"
"Yep. The drivel in these pages doesn't seem quite so bad after a good run, when you have a nice view to look at."

Not exactly earth-shattering conversations, are they? But while planning this article I realised I could use this old man to add some drama to the idea. So I upgraded his speaking part. Because the man isn't identifiable, giving him these extra lines wasn't a problem. Of course, you don't actually have to bump into someone in the first place. There have been times when I've created somebody for an article, just so I could have a conversation with them.

Do you remember this opening from an earlier chapter in the book?

"Earthquake!" shouts a young lad to his geology classmates. Playing for laughs, he falls off a small rock and collapses into fits of laughter. His friends join in with their own mock-tremors, but soon get back to their lesson, standing beside the crisp, cool waters of the stream. As classrooms go, Carding Mill Valley, with its rugged hills and beautiful beck, beats any I was ever schooled in.

The dialogue wasn't true. I made it up. However, if you go to Carding Mill Valley during school term time you will see school children being taught geology, and you will see them mucking about in the stream. That's all true. I simply used the dialogue to add a bit more interest to the piece.

With creative non-fiction, some writers will use a technique called *compositing dialogue*. This is where a longer conversation is summarised, but written as if it had been spoken that way. Some journalists do this a little, by removing all of the *umms*, *ahhs* and repetitions from a direct quote. When interviewing someone face to face, or over the telephone, interviewees may be nervous and stumble when they say things, but this is all ironed out by the reporter.

However, true composite dialogue is where a writer takes a much longer piece of conversation and summarises it, or brings together several different conversations (which perhaps take place over a period of time) into one. Composite dialogue still conveys the truth of the longer conversation.

What you mustn't do is put words into the mouths of real, identifiable people, otherwise you might find yourself falling foul of libel laws. But sometimes, creating someone to have a conversation with, such as a waiter, a shop keeper, or a passing tourist, can add more realism to an article. In fact, these two elements - creating scenes and using dialogue work really well together for some articles, such as travel pieces.

Point Of View

When it comes to point of view, journalists tend to report an omniscient overview of a story. They're trained to give both sides of a story so that the reader can make their own judgment about who they feel is in the right. Creative non-fiction can use a technique where it describes the events from one person's view point. By interviewing the person who experienced an event, a writer can learn so much about how they felt and what they endured, that it's possible to write up the story as if the writer was the one who experienced it.

This is what ghost writers do. They interview a celebrity and then write their *auto*biography for them, in a way that makes the reader feel that it is the celebrity who has written the book. And if you scrutinise some of the real life stories in the women's magazines you may see (in font 2, near the spine of the publication) the phrase *as told to [writer's name]*. This means that the writer has interviewed these people, and then written up the account as if they were the interviewee.

One reason this happens is because not everyone is great at putting their thoughts and experiences into words. We writers like to think we have word skills and are therefore better placed to recount someone's story on their behalf. So even though it turns out that it wasn't the celebrity who actually wrote their autobiography, their true story is still being told. The truth about their life is being conveyed.

Now, some people might argue that what one person believes to be true is actually a misconception, or a misunderstanding. That's how arguments happen, when people interpret things differently. However, some creative non-fiction writers take the attitude that if it's what that person believes, then what happened is that person's truth.

Let me explain that a bit more. I used to work for a high street bank and part of the induction process included safety training about what to do during a bank raid. Obviously it's important to remain vigilant during a raid so that bank staff can give police accurate descriptions of the thieves. As part of that training process we had to watch a video of a dramatised bank raid. We were told to be as observant as possible. Afterwards, we had to answer a series of questions, such as:

- What colour shoes were the robbers wearing?
- Was the gun held in the robber's right, or left hand?
- What type of jackets were the robbers wearing?

Even though we'd all watched exactly the same video, we couldn't all agree on an answer. Yet if we'd been asked to stand up in a court of law, and swear on the bible, we would have been convinced that the answers we were giving were the truth, because that's what we believed to be the truth.

So, stepping into someone's shoes and writing the events as they witnessed them through their eyes can be an interesting way of getting a better understanding of how someone thinks, or why they reacted to something in the way that they did.

This is not a common technique for articles, although it is useful for writing the real life stories of people who are not proficient at writing.

The Writer As Primary Source

You are the primary source when it comes to writing anything that you have personally experienced. It falls into creative non-fiction because journalists don't normally put themselves into the news stories. But, when Tom Wolfe went off researching for his hot rod car racing feature for *Esquire*, he realised that because he was witnessing the event, he was a primary source. He could draw upon his own senses. His journalistic instinct was to interview people to find out what it felt like to sit in the spectator gallery and watch these machines roaring along the track. But he didn't have to interview people, because he could experience it for himself.

So whenever you're writing anything where you're drawing upon your own personal experience, remember that. Remember your senses. Bring them all into your account. If you were there, then you know what it felt like. Whenever you experience something you might use in an article, jot down what your senses are telling you:

- What can you see? Sight is our most dominant sense and it's what most writers automatically draw upon when describing something. But make a point of looking for the smaller details. Often it is the smaller details that convey more to the reader.
- What can you smell? Ideally, focus on your sense of smell first. Aromas are evocative, and the mention of a smell that most of us have experienced will soon have us recalling it in our imagination. However, our sense of smell is most receptive when we first walk into somewhere. If you've ever walked into the perfumery section of a department store you'll know that overwhelming clash of different fragrances that assaults your nose all at once. Stand still for ten minutes and you'll hardly notice it, because you've got used to it. So record what you can smell as soon a you are aware of it.
- What can you taste? This isn't just for those travel articles when you're reviewing a restaurant. You can taste things on the air. You can often taste the salt on a coastal sea breeze, or the coal dust in the air at a mining museum.
- What can you hear? Rarely is somewhere completely silent. There are background noises to be heard most of the time. Think of *hernia*! As I'm writing this, a blackbird is chirping its alarm call, probably because

next door's cat is watching, and I can hear the regular ticking of the clock on my wall. Sounds are important.

- What can you feel? Is it warm, or cool where you are? Do you feel safe? Do you feel secure? Do you feel silly?

By drawing upon all of your senses you're bringing the whole experience to your readers. And this will show in your writing, because it will have authority. It will be clear to the reader that you know what you're talking about.

With many personal experience articles you'll want to come across as an expert. You'll want to be seen as someone who has been there, done that, and therefore knows what they're talking about. Draw upon your senses, and your reader will respect you for the primary source that you are.

Creative non-fiction is a huge subject area. There are many books devoted to the topic. But I just wanted to mention it in this book, because it can be a useful way of creating interesting and informative articles. The whole point of writing articles is to inform and entertain readers, and sometimes, taking a creative non-fiction approach can make the difference between a good article and a great article.

Chapter Nine

Editing

Brilliant! We have our first draft written, so it's time to relax. Well, sort of. I'm a firm believer in putting your work aside for a few days, if you can. Your brain will benefit from the break, which means when you look at it again it will be with fresh eyes.

This is why I like having several projects on the go at any one time. When I've finished drafting one piece I can put it to one side, because I have other pieces that I can then turn my attention to. But when the time comes for editing, what actually needs doing?

The first thing I do is consider my word count. How close/far away from my target word count am I? The reason I do this at this stage is because it tells me how ruthless I need to be. If I'm 500 words over, then entire paragraphs need culling. Then I can move onto the next stage of scrutinising individual sentences and phrases, which is what I would do when I'm fewer than 150 words over.

I rarely find myself needing to add to an article because I've written something too short, and this is because of the outlining process. I'm aware of how much material I need for the rough word count that I'm aiming for, so if I think my outline is too short I resolve the problem at this stage, before beginning the article.

Analysing Paragraphs

I read each paragraph on its own, as a single entity, and then I ask myself four questions:

1. Does the paragraph deal with one main point?

Ideally, paragraphs should focus on one point or argument of your article. For me, this usually relates to a bullet point in my outline.

2. What is that point?

Does that point tie in with the bullet point in my outline? Have I written what I wanted to write? There have been times when I've looked at my outline and misinterpreted what I was planning to say.

3. Is this point pertinent to your article?

Thinking about your readership and your target publication, is the point you're making in this paragraph important for your article? If it isn't, delete it. There are times when I'll look at the outline and see that the point is worth making, but to meet the space requirements of my target market, it may be necessary to question whether the point is *vital* to this particular article. This can be a tough stage of editing, because deleting paragraphs can have an impact on other paragraphs, particularly if you repeat words or phrases in subsequent paragraphs that you explain, or define, in a paragraph you're deleting.

4. Is it in the right place?

I'm also thinking about structure too, throughout this process. If the paragraph deals with an important point that I feel is right for this article and this readership, I consider whether the paragraph is in the right place. Again, the outlining process usually sorts out these structural points, but sometimes comments made in other paragraphs can mean that your piece would have a better, more cohesive argument, if a paragraph, or two, were swapped, or moved around.

I see this stage as my big movement editing. It's where I make the most drastic cuts and changes during my editing process. After that, I read through the article again, ensuring it all still makes sense, before moving onto the next stage. Then comes the smaller detailed stuff.

Adverbs

Adverbs are words that describe, or modify, an adjective, verb, or another adverb. They often describe how something is being done, or show how much or little of something there is. For example, in the sentence:

Matthew drove the car erratically

… the adverb *erratically* is describing *how* the car was being driven.

In the sentence:

Sarah was very relieved when Matthew parked the car

… the adverb *very* is describing *how* relieved Sarah was.

There are some adverbs that don't add anything to your text's description, except another word. Often these are known as *intensifying adverbs* because they're used to heighten the meaning of the verb or adjective they're placed next to. In the example above, *very* is used to intensify how *relieved* Sarah was, but it's a weak way of doing this. How do you quantify *very*? What extra relief does it demonstrate? The reader will still understand the sentence if you cut *very* from it. So is *very* needed in the first place, if the reader still understands what is being said?

In fact, that's a good rule of thumb to take with any editing. If your text still makes sense, and the message you're making to your reader remains clear after you've cut something from it, then that's a good sign that what you've cut wasn't needed in the first place.

Common intensifying adverbs that can be deleted include *very, really* and *quite.*

There are times when a verb and an adverb can be replaced by a stronger verb. Instead of writing:

Susan walked quickly round the supermarket

... you could write:

Susan dashed round the supermarket.

That's cut the total word count by one, and it's also improved the description of how Sarah hurried around the supermarket.

I should point out that adverbs are not bad words to be avoided at all costs. In fact, you can't avoid adverbs, because they're immensely useful in our work. They have just as much right to be in our text as any other word, because they help with comprehension. For example, in the sentence:

The exam takes place tomorrow

... *tomorrow* is an adverb explaining when the exam takes place. If we were to delete it we would be left with a sentence that does not make sense. So adverbs do have a place in our work, but keep a look out for the intensifiers, because they're the ones you may be able to replace with a stronger adjective or delete altogether.

Active And Passive Sentences

As a rough rule, active phrases and sentences are shorter than passive ones. What makes them active or passive depends upon whether the subject of the sentence is doing the action, or having the action done to them. Most simple sentences have three elements: a subject, verb and an object.

Matthew stole the camera.

In this sentence the subject is *Mark*, the verb is *stole* and the object is *camera.* It's an active sentence because it is the subject, *Mark*, who is doing something to the *object*, the camera.

To write this sentence passively it needs to be rephrased as: *The camera was stolen by Mark*. In this sentence the camera is mentioned first, and it is having action *done to it* by Mark.

The active version (*Matthew stole the camera)* is four words, whereas the passive version (*The camera was stolen by Mark)* is six words, so active sentences can be shorter. Active sentences are also more immediate and easier to understand.

However, that does not mean active sentences are better than passive sentences. It all depends upon which element is most important in the sentence. Readers put more importance on what comes first in a sentence. So in *Mark stole the camera* the reader will place more importance on Mark. Whereas in *The camera was stolen by Mark*, we're putting more emphasis on the camera. Here's another example:

Thieves stole the Crown Jewels.

This is active, and because *Thieves* comes first in the sentence the reader places more importance on them. Whereas, *The Crown Jewels were stolen by thieves* is passive. It puts more importance on the crown jewels. So the active sentence makes the thieves more important than the crown jewels, whereas the passive sentence places more emphasis on the crown jewels. There's no right or wrong here. It all depends upon what you as a writer want your readers to focus on.

So if you're looking to cut a few words from your text, rewriting passive sentences into their active form might be useful, but remember that doing so also changes how your text will be interpreted by your reader.

Pet Phrases

At the end of the day, when all things are said and done, we all, in a roundabout way, have our own pet phrases. (See what I did there?) Many magazine articles have a light, chatty style and, as such, they're written in a similar style to the way we talk. Because of that, it's easy for those words and phrases that litter our dialogue to litter our text too. Delete them.

The first sentence under the Pet Phrases heading is 24 words. However, if I delete the unnecessary phrases, I'm left with the core of the sentence, *We all have our own pet phrases*, which is seven words. Pet phrases can bump up your word count considerably.

There are also other phrases and clauses you might use in your article that sound good but could be said more succinctly. Instead of saying *At this moment in time* (five words), you could say *Nowadays*, or *Now*, depending upon the context, which is only one word.

Some writers feel that cutting these words cuts our voice from the piece. Style is part of writing, and I would like to think that this book has been written in a light-hearted, chatty style and that my voice has come across, too. Part of that voice includes using some of my own pet phrases. But, although I made a decision to retain some pet phrases, there were many more that I cut during the book's editing process. So don't feel that you have to obliterate every pet phrase that you come across, but be realistic. It goes back to the point raised earlier, if you can delete it from your text and what remains still makes sense, then was it really needed in the first place?

Have A Clear Message

The whole point about writing is to convey a message to our readers in a clear, simple, unambiguous way. This is something to remember during the editing process.

When you study your target market you'll get a feel for the publication's style, which includes the length of the paragraphs, the length of the sentences and even the lengths of the words. Simple words are more easily understood. The reader has less work to do to process and interpret the information.

However, explaining something using simpler words often involves using more words, so if you're looking to cut your word count, using simpler words may seem a backwards step. It all depends upon who your target reader is. Generally, words of three syllables or fewer are simpler to understand.

To give an extreme example (just because I like the word, and try to use it whenever I can), why use *floccinaucinihilipilification* when you could say *estimate something as being worthless*?

Many word processor programmes offer statistical analysis options, usually as part of the spelling and grammar tools, that assess the readability of your text. Microsoft Word will tell you:

- the percentage of passive sentences,
- the Flesch Reading Ease (score out of 100 - experts say aim for 60 to 70),
- the Flesch-Kincaid Grade Level - American - aim for about 8.

The Flesch Reading Ease is a system that scores your text out of 100, so the closer it is to 100, the easier it is to read. However, scores of between 90 to 100 are better suited to beginner readers, so for a general adult readership, aim for between 60 and 70.

The Flesch-Kincaid Grade Level measures the reading level of a student, based upon what a student at certain grade levels (in the American school system) would be expected to read and understand.

Use these as a guide. Don't be obsessed by them. If your text achieves a Flesch Reading Score of 59, don't spend hours trying to increase it to 60. But if you have a lower score then it's an indication your text may benefit from further simplification. This is where identifying passive sentences can be a useful exercise.

It's possible to encounter problems even with simple text. Remember, your work needs to be unambiguous too. Simple words can still confuse the reader. Have you written what you really meant to say? For example, in *The lady hit the man with the umbrella,* did the lady hit the man who was carrying an umbrella, or did the lady use an umbrella to hit the man?

Newspaper headlines can fall into the ambiguity trap:

Stolen painting found by tree. (Did a tree find a stolen painting, or was the painting found lying beside a tree?)

Red tape holds up new bridge. (What? There's no cement, just red tape?)

If a sentence has more than one interpretation, rewrite it so it only has the meaning your want it to have.

Read It Aloud

There's a lot to be said about reading your work out aloud. I believe that when we read work out aloud we're using a different part of our brain, because we have to read what's on the page and then convert that into speech. I don't know if we do use a different part of our brain for this process, but I can see how we have to concentrate carefully on what we're reading, because we're going to say it out loud. This probably forces us to read more slowly, reducing the chances of us skim reading, and reading what we think *ought* to be on the page, rather than what is *actually* on the page.

Saying your text out aloud has other benefits. Sometimes we hear problems we don't see. A great example is word repetitions. Words that are repeated within the same sentence, or concurrent sentences should be avoided. The repetition draws the reader's interest away from the message you're trying to get across. Read the text on paper, or on the screen, and you may not spot them, but when they're said out aloud, we hear the same sounds of the repetition more clearly.

Also, if a piece of text is easy to say it's easy to read, too. And reading your work out is a great way of spotting those times when entire words are missing from your text.

Read any book on grammar (and I would strongly advise you to have a few on your bookshelf to which you can refer on a regular basis) and you'll often read sentences where they say, "*Even if you don't know what's grammatically wrong with the sentence, you'll know that something is wrong because it doesn't sound right.*" Our ears are great at picking up grammatical problems.

You may find reading your work out aloud is embarrassing, particularly if there are other people in the house, but try it. It's surprising what it can reveal. Personally, I don't think there are any shortcuts to this bit. My computer has accessibility options that enable it to speak a piece of text, but I find it's not as good as when I read out my work aloud myself. My computer doesn't know when to breathe properly. It can help to identify missing words, but because the tone, inflection and delivery is constant, I don't pick up as many errors listening to my computer's voice, as I do when listening to my own. I clearly like the sound of my own voice, then.

Final Editing Points

When you've gone through your text several times, make sure you look out for the following:

1. Correct language spellings.

Have you used the right spelling for your market? Have you

used American spellings for a North American market and British spellings for a British market? How does your target publication deal with *ise/ize* words? Should it be *specialise* or *specialize*? (My Oxford English Dictionary tells me that *ize* has been used in English since the 16th century, and although it is widely used in North America, it is not an Americanism. The *ise* ending is more common in British English, because it reflects the French influence on our language.) So check you've used the right form of spelling.

2. Have you used the right tense?

I say this because, when recounting memories, we often start writing in the past tense knowing that we're referring to something that has happened in the past. However, as we start reliving the memory it's easy for us to switch to the present tense, because we feel as though it is happening now. Go through your text to check you've used the right tense at the right time.

3. Have you adopted the magazine's style?

Don't get paranoid about this, but if your target publication has a style guide on its website, then it's worth spending a couple of minutes applying it to your text. The style guide explains how that particular publication prefers to do things. The most common points to look out for are:

- speech marks - single, or double?
- numbers - common practice is to spell numbers from one to ten, but use numerical digits for 11 and above.
- Abbreviations and acronyms - Do they prefer full stops, or nothing? (B.B.C. or BBC?) Should it be all capitals, or just the first letter? (NATO or Nato?)
- When should you hyphenate? (e-mail, or email?)

You're not going to be rejected purely on the basis of failing to follow a style guide. Not every publication makes its style guide publicly accessible, anyway, but if you're looking to develop a good relationship with a publication it's worth getting to know their preferences, if they make them known to you.

Hopefully, having gone through all of those stages, you now have an article that conveys all the points you wanted it to, in a clear, unambiguous manner, and it meets the desired word count, Congratulations! You now have an article.

Chapter Ten

Photographs

I'm not going to go into a lot of detail here, because I do that much better in my book *Photography for Writers* (plug, plug … well, you can't knock a man for trying). But, I do want to mention the basics, because I think photographs are something that article writers should consider providing alongside their words.

Look at any magazine article and you'll find that 99.999999% of them are illustrated. (There are bound to be some technical journals, or small presses that don't, but the vast majority of publication use photos.) In fact, photos form part of the page furniture that accompanies an article.

I like to supply photos with my articles because most editors appreciate it. Editors have skills at editing words, so if they think they can improve my text, then all it takes is a matter of minutes for them to make the necessary tweaks. What takes ages to sort out are finding suitable images. By giving them some photos, or pointing the editor in the right direction where they may find suitable images, I'm making the editor's job much easier. That makes my work more appealing.

If an editor has a page that needs filling at the last minute and they have two potential articles, one with pictures and one without, most will choose the illustrated article. I believe magazine article writers increase their chances of publication if they can offer photos. Indeed, I know of pitches of mine that were successful, purely because of the example photos I submitted at the same time.

You don't need a flashy camera. Today's compact cameras are more than capable of taking publishable photos these days, so perhaps you could use the money earned from selling an article to buy one. It could be a useful investment. There are some useful tips about taking better photos, and getting the most from the different shooting options many compact cameras offer, on the website that accompanies *Photography for Writers*, which you can find at: http://photography-for-writers.blogspot.co.uk.

Analysing The Images

It's worth taking a few minutes to analyse the photos and other clues in your target publication. First, check out the bylines and credits. If you see that the articles are credited with *Words by [writer's name] Photos by [photographer's name]* then you know that the publication will use articles where the writer only provides the words. Some publications have a pool of freelance photographers that they can call upon, or they have access to online image libraries and other image resources.

However, if you note that all the main articles are credited as *Words and photos by [writer's name]* then you know that this publication prefers using writers who can supply the complete words and picture package. Remember, I'm only suggesting this as a guide. I'm not saying that if all the articles are written by writers who supply both the words and the photos that you shouldn't send your words-only article to this publication, but you may be making life harder for yourself if you do. No editor is going to reject the best article idea they've seen in many months purely because the writer can't provide the photos. (And there are always ways and means of obtaining photographs, which we'll look at later on.)

So, once you have a feel for whether the publication prefers to use writers who can provide both words and photos, take a look at the photos you see accompanying the articles in your target publication.

How Big Are They?

How big are the photos you see? Travel articles might begin with a photo that stretches across a double-page spread. Sometimes these visually stunning images are acquired from tourist boards, if the writer is unable to provide them. And remember, the first photo on a travel piece has to be stunning enough to draw the reader in.

Magazines also use many more images smaller than this, ranging from half a page down to a couple of inches square. These are all images that could be captured on an ordinary compact camera.

Blue Sky Thinking?

This tends to be a travel article issue, but look at the skies in the photos. Are they all blue? If so, then you know you need to supply blue sky photos. Most travel articles want to inspire a reader to go there, and nothing does that better than a photo with blue sky in it.

Blue skies are market dependent. For example, a walking magazine read by serious walkers won't be bothered about blue sky images. Their readers are more likely to go out in all weathers, so are more than happy to see images with grey skies.

People Present?

Are there people in the photos? Or are the photos people-free? It's an indicator to look out for. Does your target market use images that are packed with people, or do they prefer images with just one or two people in them? Sometimes people are useful to help add scale to your image. If you were writing an article about a huge waterfall, then taking a photo that has a couple of average-sized adults in it will give the reader a better sense of scale than a photo without people in it.

Also, be aware that any people appearing in photos need to be properly equipped, if they're undertaking an activity you're writing about. So when I take photos for the walking magazines, I ensure that any people in my images are wearing proper walking boots, or shoes, and suitable outdoor clothing. An article about long distance running shouldn't have people wearing high heel shoes. Cyclists should be wearing helmets in cycling magazines, for example. You'll probably pick up any specific clothing requirements from the images you see in your target publication.

White, Or Negative, Space

Some magazines use photos, or part of a photo, as a background image to the text. To do this, they need sections of the photo to have a uniform colour, or a shade that a contrasting colour be applied to easily. It is common for blue skies to be used as a placement area for text, for example. If you spot your target publication uses photos like this, then review your photos to see if you have any suitable images.

What Are The Photos Of?

Finally, look at what the photographs illustrate, and how they link in with the article. For example, if there's a photo of an information panel, is it a close up so readers can read what the information panel says, or does the photo show where the information panel is in its environment?

In an article I wrote about an interesting church I'd once visited, I mentioned the unusual font with its intricate carvings. The magazine used the close up I took showing the detailed carving. They didn't use one of the font in situ, because the close up photo illustrated my article better.

If you take your own photos, it's worth considering what you have available at the planning stage when you're thinking about the general outline of your piece. It makes sense to send in photos illustrating points you mention in your article. Indeed, if you spot your target publication prefers using images that zoom in on the references made in the article then you know you need to supply similar photos. Use your image library to help create your articles in the first place.

Submitting Your Photos

When it comes to submitting your photos, DO NOT embed them into your article document. Think back to the comments I made about boxouts and side panels. You're the writer, not the page layout designer, so where you put the photos in your article may not be where the editor or picture editor want them to go. There's also another practical point; when an image is embedded into a word processing document, the word processor will sometimes process the image too, reducing its file size so that the overall word processor document file size isn't excessive. This makes the image unusable.

Magazines need high quality images. They're printed at 300 dots per inch, which means that a one-inch square photo is made up of 90,000 dots (300 dots along the vertical x 300 dots long the horizontal). So the bigger the file size of the photo the better. Magazines can make big photos smaller, but they can't make small photos bigger.

If you have a compact camera that allows you to save your images in different quality settings, always go for the highest quality setting available. Do this and most cameras are capable of taking a one-page photo of the right quality for publishing.

Magazines use photos saved in jpeg (.jpg) format. Again, practically every camera will save photos in this file type, so it's all straight forward.

When it comes to submitting your images, save them onto a CD Rom, or alternatively you can upload them to an online storage folder where you can then give the editor access to that specific folder. (Check out www.dropbox.com or www.box.com or www.copy.com. Most offer free accounts with several gigabytes of storage space, which is more than ample. When you create a folder and upload images to it, you'll find there's an option to share the folder with someone. This will produce a link that makes no sense at all such as www.box.com/LyHnbf68o0kHGrWm, but when an editor clicks it they are taken only to this folder, and have access to everything and anything that you put inside that folder.)

When you save the photo, give it a unique reference number, and caption the photo, so the editor knows what the photo is of:

IMG_0001 - The intricate carvings on the 12th century font found at St Mary Magdalene Church, Eardisley, Herefordshire.

Giving it a unique reference number (IMG_0001) means that if you offer an editor two shots of the same thing but one in landscape format (where the longest side of the photo is at the bottom and the top) and one in portrait format (where the longest sides of the image are on the left and right) you can still determine which image is which.

I then provide a complete list of the images at the end of my article (after any boxout and further information panel text), along with details of any link required to access the folder online, if I'm not submitting them on CD Rom.

If I'm supplying images via an online folder, I also put a copy of the text in that same folder too, so that everything is together. If I'm emailing an article to an editor, I'll attach the text document to the message, and I'll also put the online storage folder link in the email message.

If you're submitting your article by post (and there are still some publications who prefer this - always check out any guidelines on their websites) then save the images onto a CD Rom. I also print out a page of the images at thumbnail size, and attach this to the back of my printed article, so the editor has something they can quickly glance at, which gives them an idea of the images available on the CD Rom.

Sourcing Photos From Elsewhere

You don't have to be a photographer to be able to provide

images with your articles. There are places where you can legally obtain images for use to illustrate your articles. As I said earlier, it's finding the photos that takes time, so if you know of any potentially useful sources, simply giving the editor this information can drastically reduce the amount of time they spend looking for suitable photos.

First things first: DO NOT TAKE IMAGES FROM THE INTERNET. In the same way that a writer's words are protected by copyright, so are a photographer's photos. Helping yourself to images from the Internet could be copyright theft, unless you ask the owner for permission to use them. (And if you do ask for permission, don't be surprised if the photographer wants paying for this use … well, photographers like being paid for their creativity in the same way writers like being paid for theirs.)

There's also a practical point. Most images on the Internet are not of a high enough quality. Photos you see online are optimised for displaying on computer screens, not magazine pages, so they are not of a high enough quality for magazines to use.

There are, though, many legitimate sources of images that magazines can draw upon, which you may help an editor find. One of the best is tourist boards. If you're writing travel features, approach the relevant tourist board to see if they can give you some images, or give you a contact address that you can forward to the magazine. Tourist boards are designed to promote places, so they often have stunning photographs to attract potential visitors, and these photos can be used by magazines.

After that, consider PR (Public Relations) agencies. If your article is providing good publicity, most PR firms and agencies will offer images for free. I've written several articles about the Royal Yacht Britannia and the media department have always provided some brilliant photos, which I've been able to forward with my articles.

When you obtain images from a third-party source always check how the photos should be credited. Most will stipulate that the copyright holder needs to be quoted, which is usually the name of the company providing the images.

There are some organisations that offer access to their photographic library via the Internet, which magazines can browse and then download what they want. Sometimes these organisations will require a magazine to obtain a password and user account. Alternatively, they'll allow them to download any images they require as long as the photo is credited accordingly. If you come across one of these sites it is better to give the editor the details of the website rather than download the images you think work best. Remember, you're the writer, so you might not download the right images. (Does the editor want to use one as a double-page spread, or as the image for the front cover of the magazine?) Instead, give the editor the appropriate website address, or contact details, so that they can select the images they feel meets the style of their publication.

Never commit an editor to using certain images. Many photographic libraries charge for the use of their images, but you have no idea what the magazine's photographic budget is (assuming they have one), so always give the editor details of the potential source of photos and let them take the next step.

So if you don't have a camera, it's not the end of the world. It is still possible to supply an illustrated article if you can't take your own photos. Even though I take my own images, I always have a quick look to see whether I can find a better source of images. One of the reasons I contacted the Royal Yacht Britannia for images, despite having many of my own, is that they were able to provide better shots. As a tourist, it wasn't possible for me to go to the other side of the quay and take a photo of the whole yacht berthed at Leith Docks, whereas the media department had been able to secure that shot. They also had images of the yacht at night, all trimmed up with lights and flags: images that it wasn't possible for me to get.

By offering photos you're increasing your chances of

success. And sometimes, for those magazines that have a photographic budget, you may also increase the fee you get for your article, when you can supply your own photos. Pictures can help you to sell more words.

Chapter Eleven

Pitching

By now you'll have realised there's quite a bit of work that goes into creating an article. (Don't worry: the more you do the easier it becomes.) But still, that's a lot of work to do without any certainty whether your article will be used or not.

Writing a complete article and then submitting it to your target market in the hope the editor will buy it is known as writing *on spec*, or on speculation. If you're new to writing articles, it can make sense to produce the article first, so you know you're capable of completing an article in the first place.

When you undertake your market analysis of your target publication, check out the contents page, or the page where the publication's editorial contact details are printed. (In most cases the publication's contact details appear near the contents page or, if not, near the beginning of the publication. However, some magazines hide the contact details in the middle or near the end of the publication. For example, *BBC Countryfile*'s contact details in the issue I'm looking at are on page 84.)

When you've found the editorial contact details, check for any guidance with regards to freelance submissions. In addition to the clauses about unsolicited material discussed earlier, you may come across publications that are genuinely helpful. The latest issue of *Best of British* says, "*Articles of up to 1200 words will be considered for publication by the Editor. They should be sent either by email or on disc if possible.*" (They later go on to say that they take no responsibility for the loss or damage to any material submitted.)

What you will frequently see is the no unsolicited material phrase (*no unsolicited material accepted, or will be considered*). Some even go as far as saying: *Any unsolicited material will be destroyed.* Ouch!

So, pitching is the way forward when a publication doesn't accept unsolicited articles. However, most professional writers pitch ALL of their ideas, even to publications that do accept unsolicited material. Why? Because it saves time. When you pitch an idea to an editor there are several responses you might receive, including:

1. That's a fantastic idea. I want this for my readers.
2. No, the idea is not right for us.
3. A great idea, but I've just commissioned/published something very similar on that topic and cannot cover the topic again for the foreseeable future.
4. I like the idea, but could you write something on the subject looking at this particular angle …

Imagine you'd spent a week carefully crafting an article, getting it as perfect as you can make it, and then you'd sent it off, only to have the editor respond with point 3 - he's just bought a similar idea. That's so frustrating, because it proves your market analysis was right, and that you'd correctly identified the right angle of your idea for the publication's readers. Unfortunately, another flipping writer got there before you. Writing the article in full was a waste of time. If you'd pitched the idea, you may have had your answer without going to all of the effort of writing the article. (Or, you might have got your pitch in before the other blooming writer did, and secured the commission.)

Likewise, point 4 has happened to me a couple of times, where I've pitched an idea and the editor liked it, but wanted something a little different. On one occasion I'd pitched a 900-word (one page) idea, but the editor came back and said he wanted two pages (1700 words) on the subject. Knowing an editor wanted 1700 words is far better than looking at a 900-word article and wondering how best to expand it to 1700 words.

So pitching is the best way forward. It's what the professionals do and it saves time in the long run. Don't be worried about your idea being stolen. This doesn't happen. What does happen is that writers have similar ideas, and if an editor commissions one they'll have to reject the others. Then, when the others see the commissioned article in print they think their idea has been stolen. This isn't the case. Generally, the other writer got in first with the idea, or their angle was better targeted at the publication's readers. (Believe me, you are not the only writer pitching Christmas-themed ideas to editors in June.)

The best response from a pitch is an editor formally commissioning you to produce the article. Usually, the editor will reply confirming they like the idea, explaining any requests they have (perhaps regarding word length, or angles) and, hopefully, mentioning payment.

You may get a slightly different response. One that says they like the idea, and they're happy to take a look at the complete article before they'll make a final decision. It's up to you what you do here. Professional writers would expect the editor to give a firm commission if they like the idea. Indeed, why should a professional writer go to all of that effort of producing an article if there's still a risk it could be rejected. The professional writer could still be wasting their time.

Personally, I take the attitude that it depends upon your circumstances. If you're new to writing articles and are trying to get your first piece published, you might want to take this risk. You know you're not completely wasting your time because the idea obviously works well for your target publication's readership. (Editors get inundated with ideas and queries, so they don't ask to see material that is of no interest to them.) It means your market analysis was good, as was your angle. But you should understand that if the editor has only asked to take a look, then that is not a firm commission. Your work could still be rejected.

If there's a particular market you're trying to break into, you might want to take this risk. There have been a couple of times when I've pitched an idea to an editor, and because I was keen to have work published in the magazine, I offered to supply the full article for the editor's final consideration, if the idea was of interest. So far, that approach has only led to one rejection, but it has led to many, many more acceptances, and has got my foot in the door of several publications.

Ideally, your pitch needs to answer THREE key questions:

1. Why is this article going to be of interest to this readership?

2. Why does this article need to be written now? (Which issue are you targeting, and why?)

3. Why am I the best person to write this article?

Now you understand why pitches are important, let's take a look at how to go about putting one together …

Get A Name

The first thing to do is find a specific name to address your pitch to. This is where your market analysis comes in handy again, because the information is in the editorial contacts section of your target publication.

It's also where it gets interesting, because some publications have many editors, whereas others have only one. If there's only one editor then that makes life easier. For publications with more than one you need to identify the best person to approach.

Editor At Large

Avoid these. They tend to be the editor at large of more than one publication, so they're overseeing the general direction of the publications, and tend not to be involved in the day-to-day running.

Editor
Usually a good bet, unless there are several other editors listed in the contacts section.

Deputy Editor/Features Editor
These can be good starting points, particularly a *Features Editor,* whose job it is to put together the main features section of the publication.

Commissioning Editor
Wahay! It doesn't get much better than this. Clearly, a commissioning editor's job involves commissioning writers. The fact that a magazine has a commissioning editor also proves that they use freelance written material.

Section Editors
Sometimes you may be better off approaching the editor of the section of the magazine your piece will best fit. Some magazines may have a travel editor, a finance editor, a health editor, a gardening editor etc, so if your article idea will work best within a specific section then approach the section editor. Sometimes these people are freelance themselves, and may not have the authority to commission, so they'll either tell you, or they may forward your pitch onto the relevant person.

Some magazines use job titles to make positions sound grander than they really are. Indeed, when I had a walking column in *Country & Border Life* magazine for over six years, I was a little taken aback when in the editor's letter at the beginning of the magazine one month, the editor said, "*this month our Walking Editor, Simon Whaley, takes a look at* …" Walking editor? That was news to me.

Identifying the right editor isn't always an exact science, but if there are several, think carefully about who to submit your pitch to. If you're completely confused, look in the editorial contacts list for an office or editorial assistant and phone them. They'll tell you who to approach.

They'll usually give you the right email address too. Not all publications list individual email contact addresses in the publications, so if you can't find the email address then try the following format: firstname.surname@magazine.co.uk or firstname.surname@publishername.co.uk

This is another reason for analysing an up to date issue of your target publication, or giving the publication a call. Magazine staff do change. The turnover on some publications is frighteningly quick, whereas with others, editors seem to stay in place for many, many years. But addressing a pitch to an editor who left three years ago will not endear you to the current job holder.

Straight To The Point

When you've found the right person, then you need to draft your pitch. Cut straight to the point. Editors are busy people, and your pitch could be one of several hundred that drop into the editor's inbox today. There is no time for waffle. Do not begin by saying how you love reading their magazine and that you devour it from cover to cover as soon as it hits the newsstands. False praise is easily recognised.

There are a couple of approaches you can use:

Would you be interested in a 900-word article for your News section called *'Writing Shouldn't Be Taxing' that deals with the steps all writers should take when they make their first sale?*

Can you see how that one sentence encapsulates everything? Once the editor has read that they know exactly why I'm getting in touch and what I'm offering. It also shows I'm thinking about where in the publication it might best fit.

The other way to begin a pitch is to draw upon the techniques you might use for the beginning of your article. After all, the technique's aim is to create an engaging opening to pique their interest and drag them into the rest of your pitch, like so:

Congratulations! You've just sold your first piece of writing. Who do you tell first? Your family? Your friends? What about the tax man?

Would you be interested in a 900-word article …

Once you've hooked the editor's interest, then you can begin to expand upon your idea …

Draw Upon Your Outline

… and this is where your outline, which you created when you were exploring your initial idea, comes in handy. This succinct series of bullet points explains to the editor exactly how you will deal with your idea and angle it.

So, for the idea about writers and tax I would include the following outline in my pitch:

Writing Shouldn't Be Taxing will:

- *clarify that you can be employed AND self-employed, so if you have a day job, you should still register as a self-employed writer if you're taking your writing seriously. (I did this for thirteen years before going full time.)*
- *explain that you're taxed on profits (the difference between your income and expenditure), not income.*
- *give examples of legitimate expenditure that you can offset against your income to reduce your tax liability (I claim my Writing Magazine subscription.)*
- *show how to keep track of your income and expenditure records to make completing tax form easy.*
- *identify when to consider engaging an accountant.*

At the start of this chapter, I mentioned that an outline should answer three key questions, one of which is: *Why is the article going to be of interest to this readership?* The outline helps to answer this. Most readers of this target publication are not professional writers. They write in their spare time, or as a means of generating an extra income. That's why the first point explains that for tax purposes it is possible to be employed in a day job, but also registered as a self-employed writer too. Many of the publication's target readers will fall into this category.

It continues to explain the basics that writers are taxed on their profits, not their income, and then goes further by identifying legitimate types of expenditure that can be used to reduce your tax liability.

Advice is given to show readers how to do this in a simple way, and explains when to consider engaging an accountant. Most writers dream of hitting the big time with their novel, or screenplay, so knowing what to do when this happens is useful. Essentially, the article shows the reader how to abide by current tax requirements whilst their writing is still in its early stages of success, but gives them solid systems to manage their tax as their writing grows, and ends by offering pointers as to how to proceed to the next stage when their writing takes off.

You could almost say the outline demonstrates the journey of a budding writer through to their goal of successful professional writer.

Sell Yourself

The last thing you should do on your pitch is sell yourself. Why are you the best person to write this piece?

I began keeping tax records when I had my first sale in 1989, when I wrote in the evenings after spending my days working in a high street bank. I still use the same systems today as a full time self-employed writer. Whilst I now use the services of an accountant, following the success of my first book, my accountant has a love/hate relationship with me. He loves doing my accounts because my systems make them a breeze to do, but he hates doing them because it doesn't take him long and he can't charge me much for his time.

Remember, you're not necessarily selling your writing skills (although a well-written pitch will demonstrate these admirably), but your experience. Focus on that aspect. When I pitched the hot air ballooning article to *Country Walking* I drew upon my two hot air balloon trips. This was published eleven years after I had my first article published, but I was still only writing in my spare time. I'd had a handful of articles published by this stage, so although I didn't have a lot of published writing experience, I did have some hot air ballooning experience.

Bringing this all together provides the following complete pitch:

Dear John Smith, (name changed to protect the innocent)

Would you be interested in a 900-word article for your News section called *'Writing Shouldn't Be Taxing' that deals with the steps all writers should take when they make their first sale? With the new financial year approaching in April, it's a timely reminder that writers need to keep the taxman informed of their activities.*

Writing Shouldn't Be Taxing will:

- *clarify that you can be employed and self-employed, so if you have a day job, you should still register as a self-employed writer if you're taking your writing seriously. (I did this for thirteen years before going full time.)*
- *explain that you're taxed on profits (the difference between your income and expenditure), not income.*
- *give examples of legitimate expenditure that you can offset against your income to reduce your tax liability (I claim my Writing Magazine subscription!)*
- *show how to keep track of your income and expenditure records to make completing tax form easy.*

- *identify when to consider engaging an accountant.*

I began keeping tax records when I had my first sale in 1989, when I wrote in the evenings after spending my days working in a high street bank. I still use the same systems today as a full time self-employed writer. Whilst I now use the services of an accountant, following the success of my first book, my accountant has a love/hate relationship with me. He loves doing my accounts because my systems make them a breeze to do, but he hates doing them because it doesn't take him long and he can't charge me much for his time.

Thank you for your time. I look forward to hearing from you.

Yours sincerely,

Simon Whaley

The pitch tells the editor exactly why I was getting in touch, the topical angle of the idea (a new tax year), the way I was going to tackle the idea, and why I was the best person to write it. Then all I had to do was sit back and wait …

Keep Records

Make a note of the ideas you've pitched, who you've sent them to, and when. The last thing you want to do is pitch an idea to an editor who's already rejected it a couple of weeks ago. When you're starting out you might think that you'll remember everything you pitch, but after a while you may find yourself on a rolling programme of pitches, at which point most people's memories begin to fail.

A simple spreadsheet recording the date, editor name, magazine and basic pitch idea is sufficient to stop you from making this error. Incidentally, I also have a column on my spreadsheet detailing whether I included photos with my pitch. If I have photos available I will usually include a couple of low resolution images (and comment in the body of my pitch that I'm attaching them as an example of the images I have available). It's this data that's highlighted my pitch stands more chance of acceptance if I attach a couple of photos. That doesn't mean that pitches without photos are rejected. The *Writing Shouldn't Be Taxing* pitch did not have photos and it turned out to be successful, but that's because the magazine isn't reliant upon photography to accompany its words. (It is a writing magazine, after all.)

I also have a couple of columns on my spreadsheet to record whether the pitch was accepted or rejected, and whether I had to chase it up, because you don't always get an answer to every pitch you make.

Chasing Up

There are no hard-and-fast rules when it comes to chasing editors. Let's be honest here, if you've pitched them an idea out of the blue, which they didn't ask for, they don't have to respond. They didn't ask you to get in touch. Do you reply to every item of junk mail that comes through your postal letterbox, or every email that falls into your inbox? I thought not.

Some editors, particularly at the glossier end of the market, or those working in the national newspapers will only get in touch if they like an idea. That's because they receive hundreds of pitches every day and the simple of act of hitting Reply and typing, *Thanks, but no thanks* would take them all day, leaving them little time to do the job they're paid to do in the first place.

However, it's worth chasing up your query after a suitable amount of time, because life happens and an editor might think about getting back to you, and then their phone rings and they get side tracked. And in my experience, there are some editors who simply don't respond to the first pitch. Perhaps they think the most tenacious writers will get back in touch, and they're the sort of people they like doing business with. I don't know. What I do know is that I've secured commissions following a second or even a third chase up email, that I wouldn't have obtained had I not bothered chasing in the first place.

It's worth bearing the following in mind:

- Editors are real people, apparently. They have lives outside of the office. Some of them get holiday entitlement so they can take their kids away in the summer holidays for two weeks.
- The days immediately before and after the latest issue has been sent to the printers is the worst time to get a response from an editor. Problems arising when an issue goes to print takes precedence over everything else.
- The editor has a dentist appointment this afternoon for the raging toothache he's had for the past two weeks.

If you've worked in an office you know what office life is like. Some writers prefer pitching by telephone, because they can react to an editor's comments and perhaps turn their thinking around, changing a 'no' to a 'yes'. I think you run the risk of catching an editor at the wrong time, although you can always contact an administrative assistant and enquire when a good time to ring would be. Email pitches can be accessed by the editor when they have the time (and are in the right frame of mind) to consider them properly. I often get commissioned on a Sunday afternoon.

I tend to chase my pitches two weeks after I first sent them. I might leave this a bit longer during peak holiday times, such as the summer and over the Christmas break. Then I follow them up for a third a final time about two weeks later. If I've had no response after three attempts I take the attitude that the editor didn't like the idea. (I can take a subtle hint.)

That isn't always the end of the story though. Some editors hold onto pitches they think may be useful. I once pitched an idea in April, for the October issue of a magazine. By the end of May, after chasing twice, I'd had no response so I assumed the editor was not interested. At the beginning of August the editor got in touch, out of the blue. Another writer had let him down and he had six pages that needed filling quickly. Could I supply the feature I'd proposed back in April, and could I do it in the next 48 hours? Naturally, I agreed. But it demonstrated to me that sometimes those pitches we think fall into some black hole in the Internet somewhere can lead to commissions.

Inexperienced writers often worry that if they pitch the same idea to two magazines they might get commissioned by both magazines to write the articles. Then what? My advice is don't worry, and rejoice you got two commissions. If you've done your market analysis you'll find you'll be writing two different pieces for two different readerships. And if you find the readerships overlap, then use a different structure to your article's middle and you'll end up with a completely different article anyway.

Pitches can also lead to surprises. The pitch used here in this chapter was one such surprise. On the face of it, it failed because I was not commissioned to write the 900-word piece I pitched. The editor responded by saying that he liked the idea but thought there was more mileage in it. So, he'd have a think and get back to me. The days became weeks, and two weeks later I still hadn't heard anything. Tentatively, I sent a polite follow-up just enquiring as to whether he'd had any more thoughts about my idea. I waited for a reply. And I waited. And waited. Two weeks later I still hadn't heard anything, so I dropped the editor another line. I was a little cheeky, but I thought that was okay because the editor had bought work from me before, so there was already a business relationship between us. Thankfully, he didn't take offence at my cheekiness and responded within a few minutes, apologising for the delay. He did, though, go on and commission a 1700-word feature on the topic, and then commission five more articles on various subjects that he listed, and ended up by asking whether I had any more ideas that fitted into his series theme. I did (of course!), and that's how my Business of Writing series began in *Writing Magazine*. All that work came my way because of a single pitch.

Pitching is something many writers come to hate, because there will be many times when you hear nothing back and you wonder whether you're doing something wrong, or pitching to the wrong people. But then, suddenly, someone will get back in touch and commission you to write something. When that happens, it's one of the best feelings to be had in an article writer's day.

Chapter Twelve

Formatting Your Text

When it comes to submitting your work the best advice is to keep it simple. Let's be brutally honest here - choosing a fancier font does not improve the quality of your writing, nor does printing it on the right shade of cream-coloured paper. And these days, who's printing work out anyway, so what does it really matter?

Actually, it does matter. Because first impressions count. Writers who supply their work in a simple, clear manner will be welcomed.

The Traditional Way

There's a lot of tradition when it comes to how writers format their text, and in these days of electronic submissions many question why we still do it this way. I take the attitude that this traditional method is the way I supply my text, *unless I see any advice from a particular publication asking for something different.*

Margins

Firstly, writers were told to have good margins around their text. This was because an editor might insert instructions to their typesetters in the margins about where to place pictures and tables, and so plenty of room was needed for this. Today, editors don't make notes on bits of paper. It's done straight onto computer, so why keep the wide margins? Tradition.

I set my margins to be an inch at the top, bottom, left and right, which isn't too wide, but it's still useful to me when I print out my text to edit it. (Yes, you'd be surprised the number of mistakes you can pick up when looking at something on a piece of paper, instead of a computer screen.)

Double Spacing

Then writers were told to double-space their text. This puts a blank line between each line of text. If you don't know how to do it, look it up in your word processor's help section. You will usually find the option in the formatting section of your word processor. Whatever you do, don't get to the end of a line and then press the Return key twice, because that messes up things considerably. Most word processors will then start the next line of text with a capital letter, because it thinks this is the start of a new sentence, when it may be the middle of a sentence. And when it comes to editing, if you insert a few words, this will then throw everything else out of kilter. Set up double-spacing at the start of your document (even better, create a template, which you use for every writing document) and you'll be sorted.

Why do we double-space? Again, it's traditional. When editors and publishers received a printed manuscript they would use the space between the lines of text to make copy-editing and proofreading amendments. This is still useful for those times when you edit on paper. But from a business perspective, copy-editing isn't done on sheets of paper these days. The original text is altered directly on computer.

So why do we still do it? Well, it makes the text easier to read, whether we're looking at it on paper, or on a computer screen. It's easier to concentrate on text that has lots of white space around it. If you're an editor reading hundreds of submissions every day, anything that makes the physical act of reading has to be useful.

And there are still times when writers are asked to provide text in this format. All of my non-fiction book proposals that I submit to publishers have been in double-spaced text, because that's what the publishers have asked for.

Sentence Spacing

If you're of a certain age, and learned to type on a typewriter (as I did), then you may find yourself in the habit of pressing the spacebar twice at the end of a sentence. You need to unlearn that habit. The reason typists were taught this was because a typewriter font was a fixed size, which meant the narrow letters (l, i, t, j) took up just as much space on the paper as wider characters (w,m). Words printed by a typewriter looked s-p-r-e-a-d out. So to make it easier to see the sentences on a page, typists were taught to add two spaces after an end of sentence punctuation mark. This made the sentences stand out, making them easier to read.

This works well for typewriters, but nobody (okay, there's bound to be someone, but no publication will accept typewriter-produced manuscripts these days) submits work produced on a typewriter today. Typescripts are produced using computers, and they have fonts that only use as much space as is required for each letter. So an *m* is twice as big as an *n* and uses twice as much space. Narrower letters and punctuation marks use less space, which means only one space is needed between sentences. If you supply text with two spaces between each sentence, either an editor will ask you to remove one of the spaces, or some poor soul in the editorial office will have to do it. (And by the time they've finished doing that, your request to be their social media friend will be ignored.)

You may surprise yourself how often extra spaces creep into your text, especially between words and sentences. It's something to consider when editing your work. Extra spaces can be added inadvertently when substituting, cutting or insert text, without realising.

The solution is to turn on the facility on your word processor that displays non-printing characters. So, things like spaces, carriage returns, tabs and indentations are all identified with a distinctive mark, usually in a different colour to your normal font colour, so they stand out. Most word processors have a button that toggles this facility on or off, and it looks like a back-to-front P. (The symbol's technical name is a pilcrow, for those of you who are interested.) Try it. Some writers like having it switched on all of the time, but I find it distracting. I only use it when I'm checking for errant non-printing characters. (If your formatting doesn't look right and you can't work out why, hitting this button might provide you with an answer.)

Font And Font Size

Plain and simple fonts work best. Ditch the fancy fonts, including the ones that look like mock handwriting. Arial or Times New Roman are best, simply because they're easy to read. (Remember the poor editor who has to look at several submissions.)

This doesn't mean to say that you have to use these fonts when writing your text. Font choice is a hugely personal decision and you can use whichever font you like to create your text. But make sure you change it to a standard font, like Arial or Times New Roman, when you come to submit your work.

Likewise, a sensible font size to use is 12pt. Anything smaller and the editor may need to get the magnifying glass out, whereas anything bigger may force them to take ten paces backwards. Yes, okay, if you're submitting work electronically, then the editor can change all this themselves to their preferred font and font size, but if you have hundreds of submissions to read through to consider, changing the font and font size on hundreds of submissions, all takes time - and editors are busy people. Anything you can do to make their lives easier will be welcomed.

If your own eyesight isn't great and you find it easier to write using a larger font, you might find it better if you increase the zoom level of your text, rather than changing the font size. The zoom level affects how the text is displayed on the screen, not how it will appear when printed, either on paper, or someone else's screen.

Justification

Only use left justification on your text. This facility gives your text a straight edge down the left hand side of the page only, leaving the right-hand edge ragged. Many publications print text in fixed-width columns, which have straight edges on both sides, and most pages in books follow this format too, (like you can see here) so we're used to seeing text with a straight edge on both sides. However, you don't need to do this. It's a layout issue, which the magazine's production staff will deal with. You're the writer. It's your job to provide the words, not layout the text. Stick to left justification only.

Text Formatting

Keep text formatting to a minimum. Use bold and italicised typefaces as little as possible, if only from the point of view that taking such steps is applying a visual design to your text, and that may not be the visual design of your target publication.

So, to sum up, keep your typescripts simple by:

- Having sensible margins around your text. An inch (2.54cm) at the top, bottom, left and right is sufficient.
- Double-space your text.
- Use a standard font, such as Times New Roman, or Arial.
- Use a sensible font size, such as 12pt.
- Left justify your text only.

Paragraphing

I just wanted to say a few words about paragraphing, because this does have implications for publishers. There are two ways to paragraph your text: *indented paragraphing* and *block paragraphing.*

Indented paragraphing is where the first line of each paragraph is shifted further right across the page, unlike the rest of the lines in the paragraph (as in this paragraph). People often press the TAB key on the keyboard to do this. (It's best to avoid doing this, if possible, because some magazine production software doesn't 'see' tabs particularly well. It's much better if you can set up your word processor in its formatting section so that it automatically indents the first line of each paragraph by a fixed amount. Again, check out your word processor's help section on how to do this.)

Block paragraphing differs slightly, because the first line is not indented. Instead an extra blank line is inserted between paragraphs. Basically, at the end of the paragraph you press the Return key twice.

When it comes to writing articles, it doesn't matter which paragraphing system you use, as long as you are consistent throughout your text. Don't mix and match. Fiction writers should use indented paragraphing only, but article writers can use either system. You're not going to be rejected because you've used the wrong paragraphing format.

Whichever system you use you'll see they both achieve the same results: paragraphs are easier to see on the page, whether it's a printed page or a page displayed on the screen.

Hmmm, are you spotting a trend here? It's as though editors want submitted text to be as easy to read as it possibly can be. Funny that, really, eh?

Do What The Editor Says

Of course, editors are gods, so the golden rule is always: format your text in the way editors tell you to.

I submit my articles in a mixture of formats. (When I say mixture, I mean different formats to different editors, not different formats within the same article.) One editor I supply work to regularly wants text formatted in single spacing with indented paragraphing and a Times New Roman font. Another wants single spacing with block paragraphing, and any subheadings should not be bold, but be in capitals and have // at the start of the subheading. Another wants double spacing with blocked paragraphing in Arial. They all have their own preferences. I deliver what they want.

Of course, it would be easier if every publication put its preferences on their website, then everyone would know where they stood. But magazines don't do this (sometimes because they don't want to encourage freelance submissions), so we freelancers have to negotiate our way through the formatting fog. That's why I say that unless you find information to the contrary, submitting your text the traditional way - double-spaced, clear font, basic font size - is the best way not to offend anyone.

There's another reason why you shouldn't get carried away with formatting your text with lots of different fonts, font sizes, and styles like bold and italics. When a magazine cuts and pastes your text into their magazine production software, a lot of the formatting is automatically stripped out. (When was the last time you saw double-spaced text in Times New Roman, font size 12, in a magazine?) This is so the text starts off with as little design in it, allowing the magazine to apply their style and formatting.

You may come across the term MultiMarkdown, which is a way of showing how text should be formatted. Instead of making text bold, the word that should in a bold typeface has two asterisks either side of it **like so**, or if the text should be italicised it should have one asterisk either side of it *like so*. Formatting text like this makes it easier for publication software and also Internet websites to display text in the way people want it formatted. But as I've said all along - you're the writer, not the page layout designer, so don't worry about any of this. What's important is that your text is clear and easy to read. But if an editor expresses a desire for you to format text in a specific way, then make sure you follow their request.

Submitting Your Piece

When it comes to submitting your articles, it's generally done electronically these days. It's another reason why it's worth analysing the publication to find a suitable name and, hopefully, email address. Some publications will offer a generic *editorial@[name of magazine]* address, although if you can find a named person, that's better.

Be succinct. In the subject line of my emails I usually begin with the words *Article Submission:* followed by the title of my article. I like to think the editor can glance down their inbox subject headers and click on the email messages that are of interest. Hopefully, an email headed up with *Article Submission:* is less likely to be assumed as junk and sent to the trash can.

If appropriate, I may name the specific section of the magazine I'm targeting in the subject heading: *Article Submission for Great Days Out.* This can be useful for those general editorial email addresses, where more than one staff member may have access to the email account. If it helps the right member of staff open the email that's relevant to them all the better.

I treat the main message of an email as if it were a letter on a postal copy. I address the editor by name and then explain what I'm enclosing, making it clear if I'm submitting a piece they've commissioned. For commissioned pieces, there's usually little else to say, however, if I'm submitting something on spec (which is rare these days) I follow my pitch outline. Instead of saying *Would you be interested in a 900-word article* I might begin with, *Please find attached a 900-word article about* … and then continue with my pitch structure, explaining why I think the article will be of interest to the readers, what the topical angle is, and then my expertise for writing the piece.

Round off your email in a professional manner, and then attach your article. Magazines accept Microsoft Word format documents, but if you use a different word processor the safest format to save your work in and to send to the publication is rich text format. Most publications are capable of opening rich text documents.

You may come across some publications that prefer you to paste the entire contents of your article into the main body of the email message. It helps them control their computer virus paranoia, although in fairness to a publication, if they find themselves infected by a virus, it can have catastrophic consequences. So if a publication's guidelines state that no attachment will be opened (because it's the opening of the attachment that launches any lurking virus) there is little point in attaching anything. I've seen some guidelines state that any emails with attachments will be deleted without being opened. So don't even waste your time. Do what they ask.

Begin your email professionally, and then after you've signed off, paste the text of your article underneath. This is another reason for not getting too carried away with different formatting options in your text. It's the recipient's email software that determines how text is displayed, so you could spend hours getting the formatting right in your email software, completely oblivious that at the magazine's end they use plain text display, which ignores any formatting options.

Do read through everything before you hit *Send.* Mistakes and typos in the covering email don't look good. And if attachments are allowed, make sure you've attached everything you've said you're attaching.

If you're using the old fashioned postal method, and some magazines still accept these, then draft a succinct cover letter explaining to the editor what you're enclosing. If you need the document or any other enclosures returning then make sure you enclose a self-addressed envelope with sufficient postage. If you don't need material returning, then it's best to ask the magazine to drop you an email with their decision.

When you've pressed *Send* or popped your work into the post box, congratulate yourself on having made a submission. Then start work on the next article.

Chapter Thirteen

An Example Article

I think we've now reached the time to show you another article of mine in full. This piece was published in an American magazine, and I was extremely fortunate because the editor was helpful. In fact, he was far more helpful than he needed to be. Sometimes you just strike lucky. Let me explain.

I'd pitched an idea to this editor about the Lake District, in particular lakes that you can walk around. The editor replied that he was keen to do a piece on the Lake District, but not all of his readers were walkers, so the walking angle wasn't right. Could I come up with something else?

He didn't have to do this. He could simply have rejected me, but he didn't. I think it was because I'd earned his respect. I'd been trying to get hold of a couple of copies of the publication so that I could undertake my usual market analysis. Whilst the magazine had a website that sold back issues to the public, it was geared towards a public living in America. The website wouldn't accept my British address, so it wouldn't let me order any back issues. Stumped, I'd contacted the editor, stating why I wanted the back copies, and asking if there was any way I could buy some. He replied, saying that he liked my attitude and determination to get to know his readers, and if I gave him my address he would pop a couple of copies in the post to me free of charge. You can't say fairer than that.

This enabled me to begin my pitch by thanking him for sending me those back issues. Perhaps he remembered me because of that. I'm not sure. However, as I read the editor's response I realised that he was right. Despite my analysis, I hadn't fully understood his readership. These people didn't mind going for a bit of a wander, to stretch their legs and get some fresh air, but they weren't keen walkers, so I needed a different sort of angle to make this idea interesting to this readership.

I'd opted for lakes you could walk around because these were the quieter lakes in the region. Read the tourist board brochures and they tell visitors to go to the big lakes: Windermere, Ullswater, and Derwent Water, where tourists can travel across these great bodies of water by boat. Aha! Suddenly, I had my angle. My Lake District article was about the lakes that *didn't* offer boat trips. So it wasn't an article about lakes you could walk around (although this is possible), for this particular readership the article was about the quieter lakes that are accessible, yet aren't swamped by coach-loads of tourists like Windermere, Ullswater and Derwent Water.

It's a subtle difference, but it's an idea that is more suited to this readership, who are keen to explore more of a region, not just the tourist honeypots. By telling them about the quieter lakes, my article was helping this readership make the most from their next trip to the Lake District. That's the angle the editor liked, and that's how this article came about. What follows is a complete copy of the text I submitted.

Contact Details:
[full postal address]
[telephone number]
[email address]
www.simonwhaley.co.uk

UNCOMMON WATERS

A 1200-word article
(plus 200-word fact file)

by

Simon Whaley

The Lake District, England's largest national park, only has one lake – Bassenthwaite Lake. All the other bodies of water are meres, waters or tarns. More than 16 million visitors explore the 885 square mile national park annually, most heading for Windermere, Derwent Water and Ullswater. All three offer boat trips and are a fantastic way to see the park's mountains and fells. One of the boat companies, Windermere Lake Cruises, carries more than one million tourists every year itself, and is the 16th most popular tourist attraction in the entire UK. Most visitors, however, miss out on the spectacular scenery surrounding the lesser-known lakes, even though they are easily accessible by car, on foot and even public transport. These 'back waters' may not have pleasure craft offering round-the-lake cruises, but they offer an opportunity to experience the real Lake District, whilst discovering some of its interesting history.

Loweswater

Lying approximately 13 miles west of Keswick, Loweswater's name comes the old Norse, *laufsaer*, which means leaves, so it's also known as the Leafy Lake. A relatively level shore-side footpath from the car park at Maggie's Bridge takes visitors through Holme Wood, a traditional English wood of alder, oak, lime, chestnut, ash and sycamore, which is the perfect home to the native red squirrel.

The western tip of Loweswater lies less than 500-yards from the national park boundary, yet on a clear, still day, the views and reflections across this mirror-like 150-acre lake are some of the best to be found in the country. Unlike all the other Cumbrian lakes, which drain away from the centre of the park, Loweswater is the only major lake that drains into the park.

For six months of the year, Loweswater is home to Hunter Davies (biographer for Manchester United footballer, Wayne Rooney, The Beatles and Lake District walking legend, Alfred Wainwright) and his novelist wife, Margaret Forster.

Crummock Water

Crummock Water is the 10th largest body of water within the park and its name derives from the Norse word for Crooked One. Lying 14 miles by road from Keswick, it's 2 ½ miles long, three quarters of a mile wide, and up to 140 feet deep. Two main sources feed the lake. One is the short, but idyllic, Buttermere Dubs stream. The other is the impressive Scale Force waterfall, one of the highest in the Lake District, with a total height of 170 feet and a single drop of 120 feet. It is widely believed that Crummock Water was joined to neighbouring Buttermere millennia ago, for the two are separated only by a narrow, half-mile strip of farmland.

Buttermere

Buttermere is a far better choice than Crummock Water for those seeking a gentle afternoon's lakeside amble. The 11th biggest lake within the park has a comfortable, relatively level, four-mile circumference. The small hamlet of Buttermere is popular with walkers keen to climb the 1,960-feet-high

Haystacks, the favourite mountain of walking legend, Alfred Wainwright, whose ashes are scattered around Innominate Tarn, near its summit.

In the early 19th century, Buttermere was the source of a national scandal, when Mary Robinson, known locally as the Maid of Buttermere (because she was the most beautiful woman in the area) unwittingly married a bigamist imposter, John Hatfield. This was only discovered when the local poet, Samuel Taylor Coleridge, wrote about the wedding in a London newspaper. Hatfield fled to Wales, but was eventually caught, before being tried and hanged in Carlisle.

Both Buttermere and Crummock Water are best approached from the east. That involves negotiating several one-in-four gradient ascents and descents through the 1,100 feet high Honister Pass, which explains why many coach tours fail to reach these magical lakes!

Esthwaite Water

Esthwaite Water is sandwiched between England's longest lake, Windermere, and Coniston Water, venue for many water speed records. Visitors often see Esthwaite Water when traveling from Beatrix Potter's house, Hill Top, at Near Sawrey, to nearby Hawkshead. Using quiet roads and lanes, it's possible to walk around this 280-acre lake, but those in the know take to their fishing boats. Esthwaite Water is the most nutrient-rich body of water within the park, making it ideal fishing for trout and pike, and the occasional passing osprey.

A young William Wordsworth, who went to nearby Hawkshead Grammar School in 1778, aged 8, enjoyed paddling in its waters. Such was his affection for Esthwaite Water that he mentions it twice in The Prelude.

Moss Eccles Tarn

Thousands of visitors go to author Beatrix Potter's home, Hill Top, at New Sawrey, yet most ignore the gentle two-thirds of a mile climb along the lane opposite to Moss Eccles

Tarn. This intimate, five-acre body of water is full of water-lilies and bordered by rhododendrons and was once owned by Beatrix Potter herself. She regularly rowed a boat on its waters to help her creative muse - which inspired her book, The Tale of Mr Jeremy Fisher, all about a gentleman frog.

Tarn Hows

Surprisingly, Tarn Hows is man-made. High in the hills between Hawkshead and Coniston, a single-track, one-way lane leads to this beauty spot, with its level two-mile path, a section of which is wheelchair friendly, surrounding the tarn. Created by the MP for Leeds, James Marshall, in 1862, Tarn Hows was originally two smaller ponds, which were enlarged and then planted with thick pine spruce and larch woodland. Today, it provides a great habitat for the red squirrel and is a Site of Special Scientific Interest because of its natural diversity. It is home to the one of the UK's rarest invertebrates, medicinal leeches, as well as the delicate water lobelia, which flowers in sheltered bays in summer.

In winter, a dusting of snow adds that special magic to views across to the Langdale Pikes and the fells of Wetherlam and Coniston. James Marshall sold the land in 1929 to Beatrix Potter. She sold half the land to the National Trust in 1930, and left the remainder to the Trust in her will.

Brothers Water

At the foot of the Kirkstone Pass, linking Windermere with Ullswater, Brothers Water is confused. It is either the Lake District's smallest lake, or its largest tarn. Named from the old Norse word, *Brothir*, which means broad, it was known as Broad Water until renamed in the 19th century, when two brothers tragically died in its waters after falling through thin ice.

Taking the level path along its western shore enables visitors to walk alongside some of the oldest oak woodlands found anywhere in the Lake District. It's also the route Dorothy Wordsworth took on Good Friday in 1802, the day after she'd spotted those famous daffodils on the banks of Ullswater. William sat nearby, writing poetry, whilst Dorothy went exploring. In her diary she wrote, "I was delighted with what I saw. The water under the boughs of the bare old trees, the simplicity of the mountains, and the exquisite beauty of the path." Today, both Dorothy and William would recognise the path along Brothers Water.

So, whilst Windermere, Ullswater and Derwent Water draw the crowds, these seven seductive shorelines offer a tantalising glimpse of the Lake District without the tourist trappings. For these uncommon waters, small is most definitely beautiful.

Watery Lake District Statistics

- Wastwater is England's deepest lake, with a depth of 258 feet.
- The boat, Lady of the Lake, operated by the Ullswater Steamer Company, was launched in 1877. It is the oldest working passenger vessel in the world.
- Coniston Water was popular for world record speed attempts because it is the longest straight stretch of deep water, devoid of islands, of any English lake.
- Ennerdale Water is the only large lake in the Lake District without a road running alongside it.
- Haweswater was created in 1929 when the world's first hollow-buttress dam was built.
- Derwent Water has a floating island that often appears at the end of summer. It's a mass of soil and decayed plants that rises to the surface on a bed of natural gasses and sinks again, when the gasses have dissipated.
- In November 2009, heavy rain caused horrendous flooding in Cumbria. The surface level of Windermere (10 ½ miles long) rose by over 5 feet, when an extra 9,900,000,000 gallons of rain water drained into it – 5,800,000,000 of which poured in within 36 hours.

- Seathwaite, a couple of miles from Buttermere, is England's wettest inhabited place, with an annual average rainfall of 140 inches.

Illustrations Available From The Following Link: [*my www.box.com link appeared here*].

IMG_1336 - Mist above a wintry Esthwaite Water
IMG_1983 - Mirror-like reflections in Loweswater
IMG_1985 - The mountains of Whiteside - Grasmoor and Mellbreak reflected in Loweswater
IMG_2070 - Reflected tree in evening sunshine at Crummock Water
IMG_2107 - Esthwaite Water - where William Wordsworth frequently paddled
IMG_2276 - Man-made Tarn Hows in winter
IMG_2281 - Tarn Hows with a snowy Wetherlam in the distance
IMG_2282 - Tarn Hows with a wintry Wetherlam in the distance
IMG_2708 - Walkers on the shore-side path of Buttermere
IMG_2716 - Fleetwith Pike on the shores of Buttermere
IMG_3445 - Crummock Water surrounded by heather-clad mountains
IMG_3463 - Crummock Water and Buttermere
IMG_3465 - Crummock Water and Buttermere
IMG_3529 - Brothers Water as seen from the wooded path
IMG_3532 - Brothers Water with the Kirkstone Pass in the distance
IMG_3546 - A fence line into Brothers Water
IMG_3678 - Water lilies in Moss Eccles Tarn
IMG_3679 - Water lilies in Moss Eccles Tarn
IMG_4297 - Moss Eccles Tarn near Beatrix Potter's home

Ends

Let's look at this in a bit more detail.

Contact Details
You'll have noticed at the start of the article, before the title, I've placed some contact details. I include my full postal, email and website addresses. Including a telephone number can be helpful if the editor has any queries they need answering quickly. This is all the information an editor needs to get in touch with me (and, more importantly, all the accounts department require so they can send me some money).

Title And Word Counts
After that, comes the title and the word counts. As you can see, I've quoted two: the article word count and then the additional word count for the fact file I've provided. I don't know if other writers do this, but I feel it makes it clear to the editor what I'm offering.

Writer's Byline
After that I repeat my name as the author of the article. If you want to write under a pseudonym, put your pseudonym here, but keep your real name in the contact details. Writing under a pseudonym is a personal decision. There's no need to do it, but it does have its uses at times. I know of writers who provide several different columns to the same magazine, so the editor puts the columns down under different pseudonyms. This gives the readers the impression that there are several different writers writing for the publication, when in actual fact there's only a handful. Some writers choose to write under a different pseudonym for different areas of expertise. While *Darcy Fetherington-Hughes* may be a great name if you write ballet features, you may feel it doesn't convey the right impression for your rock and roll band interviews. You don't have to have a different name for different genres. I don't. I write all of my articles under my name, and I also write short stories for the women's magazines under my

name. You don't have to use pseudonyms, but you can if you want to.

Introduction

I like to think that my introductory sentence states one fact, quickly followed by a more startling fact. It tells the reader I'm writing about England's largest national park, but then I hit them with the quirky information about it only have one lake. Hopefully, this startling statement encourages the reader to continue. From here, I expand upon the fact that the Lake District is one of our most popular national park destinations, and back this up with some statistics, focusing in on the three biggest lakes and tourist attractions. Then I throw in the angle of this feature: that I'm going to discuss the quieter lakes and waters, the ones that the hordes of tourists miss. This is where the reader is going to learn something new. This is what really hooks them into the main section of the article, because they're going to discover where to go that the coach tours don't go. This is what will make their trip different.

This is a long opening paragraph, but it fits the style of the publication. By the time the reader has reached the end of this paragraph they know exactly what this article is about. I may not have told them which lakes I'm going to write about (although they'll quickly see from the sub-headings throughout the article which bodies of water I'm going to discuss), but they know what they're going to learn by sitting down and reading my article.

The Middle Structure

As structure goes, there's a soft journey here. When I say soft, I mean the journey isn't obvious. I don't tell readers to start at one lake and then move onto the next. However, if you plot the different lakes on the map you'll see that I start off in the west, focusing on Loweswater, Crummock Water and Buttermere, then I come southwards to write about Esthwaite, Moss Eccles and Tarn Hows, before heading east to Brothers Water. If readers were planning a trip to the Lake

District they can see that the lakes I've mentioned have been grouped together in such a way that the west lakes could be visited in one trip, the south lakes in another trip and Brothers Water on a different day.

By focusing on seven specific lakes, I could have used a number structure here. Indeed, if you look at my ending you'll see the phrase *seven seductive shorelines*. This was my original title and the structure for my first idea about lakes you could wander around. If the editor had liked that angle I would have numbered each lake subheading. (Indeed, with a numbered structure, the number is usually included in the title.) However, because we went for a different angle the number structure wasn't appropriate, although the sub-headings still were. This works well, I feel, because the paragraphs remain tightly focused on the information I wanted to get across.

Ending

The ending I went for here is a summary ending. Although I refer back to comments made in the introduction about the three largest lakes drawing the crowds, the ending summarises why readers should consider these seven smaller lakes because they are just as outstanding as those other larger lakes.

Fact File

I offered a fact file at the end of this piece, because I'd noticed during my market analysis that a few articles in the publication had one. I think the editor would still have used my piece had I not offered one, but at least by offering a fact file I was giving the editor the option. Although readers of this publication frequently travel from the United States to the United Kingdom, the fact files used in the publication did not give travel information, but supplementary information about the article's subject matter. So I offered readers a series of watery Lake District facts about the lakes that I didn't explore in my article. The editor could have chosen not to include this, and if he had the reader wouldn't have been aware anything was missing.

Photographs
You can see how I've listed the 19 photographs I supplied with the article, at the end of the text, after the fact file. Of those 19, the picture editor selected six to accompany my article.

Images with the same caption (IMG_2281/2282, IMG_3463/3465, IMG_3678/3679) were different orientations of the same image: one was landscape, the other was portrait. The reason why my image numbers don't start at IMG_0001 is because I use the image numbers allocated by my camera at the time that I capture the shot. For me, that's the easiest way of keeping track of which photos accompany which articles.

So there's a real life example of a published article of mine that was pitched, commissioned and then written using the techniques I've discussed in this book. As you can see, though, we're not at the end of the book yet. There are still a few more points to consider.

Chapter Fourteen

Understanding Rights

In preparation for that joyful moment when an editor gets in touch to say how much they love your article and want to publish it, it's important that you understand the various rights you have in your work, and what you can do with them. I should make it clear that I'm no legal expert, and if you are faced with a publishing agreement that you do not understand then you must seek professional advice.

This is where membership of a relevant organisation pays dividends. The Society of Authors, National Union of Journalists and the Writers' Guild all offer members contractual advice, and these organisations see a variety of contracts so they know what the benefits and drawbacks of each contract are.

It's very tempting, when you receive your first acceptance, just to sign on the dotted line. Don't. You might think it's only an article, and you're being paid for it, but nobody knows what the future may bring. I mentioned at the start of this book that when you've written several articles on a particular topic you might want to consider consolidating it all into a book. In which case, you may decide you want to use your articles, word for word, in your book. But does the contract you signed with the magazine allow that?

I use the term *contract* loosely. I have signed a couple of contracts, but for many magazines the contract may only comprise of an acceptance email from the editor stating which rights they require in your work. In my experience, American magazines are better at supplying contracts that you have to formally sign and return, although more UK publications are doing this, particularly as they try to acquire more rights. Whether you sign a contract or not, make sure you know what rights you're licensing to the magazine.

Copyright

Essentially, the rights we offer to publications all stem from copyright. As soon as we create something, and put the words down on paper, or on the screen, we own the copyright in that text. It's important to understand that copyright relates to ideas that have been expressed in some permanent format. You can't copyright an idea until you express it in some way, such as writing it down on paper. Copyright does not apply to ideas discussed verbally with friends over lunch, for example.

Once you've expressed your creation in permanent form (whether it be words on a page, or taking a photograph), you own the copyright. In the European Union you do not need to do anything to formally register your copyright. The Berne Convention for the Protection of Literary and Artistic Works was an international convention established in 1896 that stipulated copyright must apply automatically and not need to be formally registered. In America there is an additional, but optional, formal copyright registration process, which enables creators to claim for statutory damages and legal fees, in addition to any other compensation they're entitled resulting from any breach of copyright.

Slowly, copyright protection is gradually being standardised around the world. Generally speaking, copyright exists for an additional 70 years after the year the creator dies. So if a copyright creator died in 2000, their work is no longer in copyright in 2071.

Copyright is important because it gives the copyright holder the right to license their work and generate an income from it. So, if you sell the copyright in a piece of work to someone else, that new owner has the right to exploit that creation, not you.

When you license your work you are giving someone permission to copy it and use it for specific purposes, usually for a fee. That's how creative people earn a living from their creations. So when you sell an article, you're not selling the article itself, you're selling a licence to a magazine giving them the legal right to use your words in their publication.

Traditional Freelance Working

In the days before computers and the Internet (remember them?) an article writer would sell first print rights in their work to a magazine for that particular country. In the UK, this meant that a writer would sell *First British Serial Rights. First* meant the publication was buying the right to be the first in that country to use those words. *British* identified the country where that first right applied, and *Serial* determined that the rights relate to being used in a magazine or newspaper.

This enabled a creator to sell several licences from the same piece of work, generating several earning opportunities from this particular creation.

In theory, when you've sold the *first* rights, you could sell *second, third, fourth* and so on rights. In practice, it was possible to sell *second* rights, which is why you sometimes see phrases at the bottom of a magazine article that says: *this article first appeared in XYZ magazine.* Because the publication buying second rights was publishing material that people may have already seen, the money generated from second rights was usually far less than that paid for first rights. (Which is why selling *third, fourth, fifth* and so on wasn't worth the effort).

But those *second, third,* and additional rights apply to that same country that you sold the *first* rights in. There was nothing stopping creators from selling first rights in other territories. The joy of writing in the English language is that there are many countries around the world that use English, opening up an array of useful markets.

Cunning creators would sell *First British Serial Rights* in an article to a British publication and then they would look to sell *First North American Serial Rights* to a publication in the USA or Canada, and then try *First South African Serial Rights, First Australian Serial Rights* and so on. And when they'd sold those *first* rights in those countries they knew they could still offer *second* serial rights in those countries if the opportunities arose.

The reason this system worked was because the readerships were clearly demarcated and distinct. If you sold the same article to a magazine in Britain and also to a magazine in North America, the chances of a reader buying both publications and reading the article were practically negligible.

Then the Internet happened, and suddenly, the world got smaller. Those demarcations between the different markets are blurring all of the time, and publishers, quite rightly, needed to reconsider which rights or licences they required when buying work from creators such as writers. For example, many magazines have a digital edition as well as a physical print edition. In the phrase *First British Serial Rights* the word *Serial* identifies a physical publication. So if a magazine bought *First British Serial Rights* from you, you were only licensing them to use your article in their print edition, not their digital edition. Most digital editions are exact replicas of the print version, so if a publication wants to use your article they're going to need you to license to them the right to use it in their print and digital version.

The Internet also means that people have access to information wherever they are in the world. This means that it is not practical to offer a publication *First British Electronic Rights*, because that would mean the publication could only sell their digital version to people based in the UK. Yet you may already know from your own experience that it's possible to buy foreign digital magazines from anywhere in the world through online sellers, such as *Zinio* or *PocketMags*. As a result, publishers often ask for more rights. This is why it is so important that writers understand how rights work.

The Three Key Components To Rights

When you grant someone a licence, or the right, to use your work, there are three key areas that you should consider:

- Territory,
- Medium,
- Time.

Territory
Rights are usually granted to apply to a specific region, or territory. That's why you could sell *First British Serial Rights*, and then try for *First North American Serial Rights* and so on. It was possible to sell *first rights* several times over, as long as they each applied to different, distinct territories.

With people being able to access information from anywhere in the world, via the Internet, a new territory has appeared in publisher's requests: *World Rights*. Grant this licence and you give the publisher the right to use your material anywhere in the world. Or *this* world, at least. In theory, you could grant someone a licence to use your material on the Moon, but I don't think the market is particularly large there at present, so there probably isn't the demand for *Moon Rights*.

Medium
This relates to the format of how your creation can be used. *Serial* related to physical, print magazines. *Book* clearly relates to physical books, and *Film* rights grant producers a licence to express your text in cinematic format. (I'm not aware of any articles being converted into film format, but it is possible for other short creative forms, such as the short story, to be developed into films, so don't dismiss anything.)

In theory, it's possible to licence the use for any medium. You could try selling T-Shirt rights, mug rights, the side of white van rights, and so on.

Time

Not all licences require a time clause. When you grant a magazine *First British Serial Rights* you're giving them a licence to use it in one issue. (They might be able to use it more than once in the same issue, but what would be the point?) If they wanted to use it in another issue, they would no longer be publishing it for the first time in Britain, so they'd need *Second British Serial Rights*.

But there are times when a timescale is required, and this often relates to a window of exclusivity. There may be a clause where the publication requires the exclusive right to use the material digitally for six months from when it appears in the print issue. This would mean that you couldn't license that same work to anyone else for digital use during that six month period.

Alternatively, you may come across requests for a licence that gives a publication the right to be the first British publication to print the article, but also want first worldwide exclusive serial rights for one year afterwards. That means you couldn't sell first serial rights to anywhere else in the world during that exclusive period. If, when that period has expired, there are some countries where the publication didn't exercise those first rights, you may then have an opportunity to exploit them again yourself.

Confused? It's easy to see why people don't like discussing the rights magazines ask for, because it can get confusing quite quickly. That's why understanding the three key components can be helpful. Knowing the territory, the medium and any exclusivity arrangements will get you to the core of the agreement.

Understanding The Impact Of Rights

The reason why you should always know which rights, or licences, you've granted in your work is because it affects what else you can do with your text. When I started selling articles, the standard licence request was for *First British Serial Rights*. Occasionally, I also went on to sell *First North American Serial Rights*. Writers like this because it means getting paid twice for the same piece of work. Why write something new when you could always sell something you've already written?

But the world is getting smaller. Publishing companies are getting bigger and becoming multi-national. Rather than buy the rights for a magazine to use your work, some publishers are trying to acquire the rights for the use of your work by any publication within the same publishing organisation. As a result, some interesting clauses can slip into licensing agreements.

For example, one publisher I've worked for on numerous occasions amended its standard contract. In this digital age, it needed to acquire licences to use writers' material in digital editions it was planning on using. When I read through the new standard contract the publisher was asking for *First Worldwide Serial Rights*. On the face of it, this seems straightforward. They want the right to be the first anywhere in the world to publish the article in question.

Being the first in the world to publish an article does not prevent me from selling *First North American Serial Rights* in the same work, once this publisher has published my article in the UK. And if it only appears in the UK, I can sell *First North American Serial Rights* to a publication in the USA or Canada, and they would be the first in that particular territory to publish the piece.

The implication of *First Worldwide Serial Rights* means that I have to hold off from selling other first serial rights until the article has been published by this particular company. (If I'd sold *First North American Serial Rights* to an American magazine and they published it before the UK company had published it, the American company would have been the first to publish it in the world, even though they were just publishing it in America, which would contravene the rights the UK company had.)

So this clause affects the timing as to *when* I can start exploiting other rights in this particular piece.

However, further down in the contract there is a clause stating they want the right to re-use my article, without further compensation, in any of the publications they or their subsidiaries published, *anywhere in the world.*

Now, there are a couple of points here, not least the clause about reusing the article without further compensation - in other words - using it again for free. Normally, I would expect to get paid something for second serial rights, so this would mean giving up any further payment from this source. However, it also impacts upon other potential markets. Because what if this publisher has an American company? They might decide to use my article in one of their American publications, as this clause gives them the right to do. This affects whether I can sell *First North American Serial Rights*, because I have no knowledge of when, or even if, the UK publisher may use the material in one of their North American publications. If I sell *First North American Serial Rights* to a North American magazine called NA Mag, but the UK publisher reuses my article and publishes in one of their own North American magazines before NA Mag has decided to publish, then the UK's North American subsidiary has used *First North American Serial Rights*, not the magazine I sold those rights to.

So, this second clause throws problems my way if I plan to sell first serial rights to other countries around the world. I'm not saying it's not possible to do this. If NA Mag publish the piece first, before the UK subsidiary reuses my article in one of their North American magazines then everyone is happy, because everyone has got what they wanted. But the potential for problems is that much greater.

Problems can arise with electronic rights too. I once

sold an article to a UK magazine and they wanted *First British Serial Rights* and *six months exclusive electronic rights*, so they could use the piece in their digital version, and have some of it on their website. I went on to sell *First North American Serial Rights* in the same article, but this magazine also wanted *six months exclusive electronic rights.* Thankfully, the North American magazine didn't need the piece until after the exclusive electronic rights had expired with the British magazine, so it wasn't a problem, but if the two pieces had overlapped, both markets could not have had exclusivity on the electronic rights at the same time.

Beware All Rights

I have seen contracts that state that the copyright rests with the author, but that the magazine is given all rights to the text in all media forever. Well, that's effectively signing over copyright. If you've licensed all rights to a magazine, then you have no rights left to license, even though, technically, you still retain the copyright. You can't do anything else with the text. If you're happy licensing all rights, that's fine, but don't be misled into thinking that by retaining copyright you still have some rights left. You don't.

You might think that nobody would sell all rights in their work, but there are times when I have, but I'm acutely aware of the implications. For example, I sometimes sell all rights in the walking route descriptions I produce. Remember, the magazine is only buying the right to use those particular words in the order that I've put them for that particular article. So, if I've written a 500-word walking route description for a five mile route around my home town, the magazine has bought all rights in those 500-words. They can use that article again, anywhere they like: in another magazine, on their website, on a smartphone app, even on a T-shirt, or on a mug, without further payment to me.

Different Words = Different Copyright

But, that doesn't stop me writing up the same walk using 500 different words, because copyright applies to how each idea is expressed. In a new article I'm expressing it differently with different words. I can also write it completely differently using 2,000 words, if I wanted, which would create a very different piece. I could even rewrite the walk by writing it in a different direction. If it was a circular walk written in a clockwise direction, I could write it again, but describe it in an anti-clockwise direction. Different words make it a different piece, and as soon as I create a different piece, I own the copyright in that piece, which gives me the right to license that as I see fit.

That's the benefit of non-fiction; it's much easier to rewrite something using different words than it is with fiction. So, going back to the company earlier who wanted *First Worldwide Serial Rights*, if I think the piece is right for them, I can sell it to them (if they want it), but there's nothing stopping me rewriting the article and creating a new article on the same topic and offering that to other publications around the world. The new article has its own copyright.

If you go back to the beginning of the book and consider what I say in the market analysis chapter, you'll see that magazines have different readerships, some more varied than others, but many want different lengths, or different styles, which essentially means different articles. Yes, it is still possible to sell exactly the same article to different publications across the world, but I'm finding that when I come across a potential foreign market, I end up rewriting the article for this particular readership, which means that I create a brand new article.

Standard Contracts Are Negotiable

I mentioned earlier that some magazines often have standard contracts. These are usually drafted by the company's legal department and have very little to do with the editor of the magazine. However, if you're offered a standard contract and there's something you don't like about it then enquire with the editor if it can be altered. Some publishers are more flexible than others.

It doesn't matter which side of the business deal you are on, the ultimate goal for both sides is to get as much as you can. The publishing companies are looking for as many rights as they can get, and the writers are looking for as much money as they can get for granting them a licence in as few rights as possible. I've been able to get publishers to change an *All Rights* contract to a *First Worldwide Serial Rights* contract. That gives me more flexibility, and in reality, the publisher still gets the main rights they're after. On the other hand, some publishers stick to their guns and dig their heels in and offer the, "Take it, or leave it approach."

It's your decision what you do. But whatever you do, make sure you understand the consequences of the licence you're giving the publisher when you sign a contract, and get some help if you don't understand it. Intellectual property rights can be a complicated matter, which is why novelists and non-fiction book writers try to engage the services of an agent to deal with this for them.

Should You Write For Free?

Which brings me onto the subject of writing for free. Should you do it? (It's at this point where I stand back and light the blue touch paper.) This is one of those topics that galvanises people onto opposing sides.

If you've created something then copyright rules exist to enable you to exploit any monetary value that exists in your creation. Giving it away for free could be wasting that copyright exploitation opportunity. As soon as people learn that writers are willing to write for free, why would anyone ever consider paying for it in the future? Do this and you begin to destroy the market not just for yourself but for every other writer who is trying to earn a living from their creations.

Giving away something for free suggests you don't value it. And if you don't, why should others? Writing articles takes time, if not just the writing process, but the research too. Writing for free puts no value on that time. And remember, if you're happy to have your work published and not be paid for it, it means you're granting a licence to the publisher to publish your work without paying for that licence.

The old adage is that nobody expects a plumber to come round and install new taps in their bathroom without them invoicing you for their time and effort, so why should people expect you to work for free?

Respect yourself. Put some value on your writing.

There are times when value for your work can be achieved without money changing hands though. I have written articles for which I received no payment, but I did get some really good publicity for my books out of it: publicity that would have cost me a lot of money had I needed to get my chequebook out. There are also times when I've written articles for local charitable organisations, or local associations, that I wanted to support, but knew they didn't have the funds to be able to pay for such material.

My attitude to this is be realistic. If it's your first acceptance and you're desperate to be published, it's understandably easy to let a magazine publish your work for free, because you want to see your name and your article in print. But ask yourself whether the publication *is capable* of paying you. If it is then ask for payment. If you've written something for the local parish magazine, which is read by fewer than fifty people and only raises enough money to cover its printing costs, then you know they're not going to have a lot of money sloshing around to pay for contributions. But if a glossy magazine wants to use your material, and the magazine is full of adverts from well-known brands, then they're in business to make a profit and should be paying for your work.

The more advertising space a publication has, and the bigger its circulation, the better placed it is to be in a position to pay for your work. They might not want to pay for it - they are a business, after all, and the best way to make a profit is to cut costs as far as possible (and free content is one way of doing that). But just because a publication doesn't want to pay, doesn't mean it *can't* pay.

I might write for free if I'm getting something out of it in return, or because it's a cause that I personally wish to support. But if a publication that I expect should be able to pay says it can't then I will withdraw my submission. If this happens to you, don't go all militant and threaten to blot their name on every social media platform you can think of. Instead, thank them politely for explaining the situation, and clarify that you're unable to offer them a licence to use your work without payment. This is not personal. This is a business decision.

I have had situations in the past when having withdrawn my work, an editor has suddenly been able to find some slack in their budget and can offer me a payment. And for those times when they can't, we've understood each other's position and parted on good terms. One thing to remember is that today's editor with no budget, could be tomorrow's editor at a different publishing company with a decent budget. Decent editors will respect your right to value your creative work.

Chapter Fifteen

Keeping Records

I don't know how good you are at keeping records but, when you begin submitting articles, it's a habit you need to develop. Hopefully, if the article-writing bug flourishes, you'll be submitting articles and pitches on a regular basis, so you'll need to keep track of everything. As we've just seen in the last chapter, when the joyful news from an editor accepting your work arrives, it's vital you record which rights you've granted them in that work, so you know which rights are still available for you to exploit.

Your system can be as simple or as complicated as you like. There's no right or wrong way; it just needs to be a system that works for you. I know of writers who use index cards, whilst others use notebooks. Some use spreadsheets and then there are the weirdoes like me who create a database especially for the job. When you've had over 600 pieces published notebooks and spreadsheets get a bit cumbersome.

Devise a system that works best for you, and consider keeping track of the following information:

1) Date of Submission
2) Publication Submitted To
3) Editorial Contact Name Submitted To
4) Submission Status
5) Payment Offered
6) Payment Received
7) Rights Sold
8) Date Published.

Most of those are straightforward, but I will explain my *Submission Status* category. I use it to identify the current stage the project is at. If I've pitched the idea to an editor it reads as *Proposal Pitched.* When I've submitted the complete article to an editor it becomes *Submitted.* If an editor acknowledges safe receipt, or I receive an automatic email response notifying safe receipt I record this too. It saves chasing an editor, enquiring whether they have received the submission.

After that come what I term the decision statuses: *Accepted* (Yay!), *Rejected* (Boo!) For rejected pieces, the process can start again, but if they've been accepted I then start recording further steps. I'll mark a project as *Awaiting Publication and Payment*, and then update with *Published* and *Paid* when that action occurs.

The reason I do this is because it makes managing my submissions easier. At first, collecting all of this data may seem a waste of time but, after a while, you'll begin to reap the benefits. I can interrogate my system and ask for a list of projects that haven't had a status change for a couple of months. This allows me to assess whether I need to chase. If a project has been at my *Acknowledged Receipt* stage for a couple of months then I won't worry about it, but if I've not heard from an editor for several months after my initial submission it may be worth getting in touch. (Email systems do lose submissions, as does the snail mail system.) Naturally, I want to keep a tight watch on when payments are due, so knowing which payments are outstanding is an important business issue.

And it's at times like this when the data you've collected becomes useful. I can interrogate my system and find out what's happened in the past. If my last few submissions to an editor didn't receive any response until three months had passed, then I don't bother chasing for any news until after three months have passed with this submission.

Likewise with payments, because I record the date I receive a payment from a publication it's possible to work out (when you've had a couple of payments from them) roughly what date of the month they make their payments run. This makes it easier to determine whether a payment may be received any day soon, or whether I've just missed a payment and need to chase.

Having all of this information to hand, in a system that works for you, will give you confidence. It's important that you know what stage your projects are at and whether you're waiting for anything to happen next. It also enables you to maximise your opportunities for exploiting all of your rights available in your work. And I know that you won't want to think about this, but because copyright lasts until 70 years after the year we die, it's worth having a system that relatives will be able to understand, because when you die you can pass on your copyright to them, giving them the opportunity to exploit further rights in your work. They can generate an income from your words after you've shuffled into that big reject tray above. (Assuming you want them to do that. If you don't, I'm sure the local cats home will be grateful.)

Expanding Your System As You Develop

My database has continued to grow as I've developed as a writer. If ever you find yourself asking a question about a submission, consider whether you need to tweak your system to enable you to collect that data. For example, I soon realised that I sold more of my written work when I could offer photos to accompany the text. (I have already mentioned *Photography for Writers*, haven't I?) One day, I was chasing up a submission I'd made to an editor (in the days of snail mail) and he confirmed that he had not received my submission, and asked me to resubmit.

It was at this point I realised I had no record of the digital photographs that I'd saved onto a CD Rom and submitted with my article. (Now you know why I also list them at the end of my article text, too.) It took me a couple of hours to go through and find the images I thought I'd included with that original submission, burn them onto another CD Rom and resubmit it with a duplicate copy of the text. From that moment onwards, I've always recorded which photographs I've supplied with every article I've submitted.

When an article is published I now also record which photographs the magazine has used, because they don't use every image I submit. There's another reason for doing this: *secondary rights*, which I'll explain shortly.

When I receive a payment I now record the payment method: cheque, BACS direct credit or Paypal. It prevents me from repeating the embarrassment of chasing for payment because there was nothing showing in my bank account, when the publication in question had paid the funds into my PayPal account. Oops!

I now use my database to record any business mileage I incur for projects. If I'm undertaking research, or going off to do a walk somewhere for one of the walking magazines, living in a rural location means I'm reliant upon my car. At the end of the tax year I simply interrogate my database to bring up all of my business trips between the two dates of the tax year, and it even gives me an annual figure.

I record every payment I receive connected with a project on my database. So for those articles where I've been able to exploit several different rights, I can see a total income figure for that project, which may stretch across many years. Whilst this information can be interesting, it's also a useful reminder that it's possible to sell articles to different markets around the world years after you first wrote them.

But I want to re-iterate that my database system has evolved over several years. There's no need to start off with anything as complicated as my system now is (although I don't think it is complicated). Create a system that works for you, but appreciate that as you develop as an article writer your system may need to grow and evolve with you. If you get on okay with spreadsheets I would recommend this approach, because it can be a simple way of being able to sort your data. And if you find yourself needing to take the next step and turn it into a database, importing spreadsheets into a database programme is straightforward, and one of the quickest ways to get a database programme up and running.

Secondary Rights

I mentioned earlier about Secondary Rights - these are additional ways in which you can receive payment for your articles, once they've been published. There are a number of collection agencies around the world who administer these payments, and in the UK it's the ALCS: Authors Licensing and Collecting Society. So where do they get their money from and what's it for?

Their income comes from many sources, but perhaps the best example is that of photocopying. Educational establishments, such as schools, colleges and universities, pay a fee to the Copyright Licensing Agency in the UK (set up by ALCS and another organisation) that permits them to photocopy, or digitally scan, published material. If a university lecturer read your article and felt it would improve their students' understanding of a subject, the fee paid by the university to the CLA gives them the right to photocopy your article and distribute the copies to the students. Similar fees are collected from other large establishments, like health authorities and government agencies. They also collect money from similar agencies around the world.

Writers who have had articles published can register their work with the agency. If you've had an article published you are entitled to a share of the money. Note that payment does not mean that your article has been photocopied, merely that it's *available* for photocopying or scanning. The more articles you've had published the bigger the slice of the pot you're entitled to. (Although it should be remembered that more and more articles are being published, so even if the distribution pot increases, it is being distributed across a greater range of articles.)

In many European countries a small levy is added to the price of copying and scanning devices that are bought for private use. These funds are passed onto ALCS and similar collecting societies around the world, for distribution to writers, in recognition of the private copying that people make of material in their own homes.

These are called secondary rights because the writer has already licensed the primary rights directly to the magazine. To register for payments you need to join and become a member, for which there is a small, one off charge, but this is deducted from your first payment, so there's no need to pay any money upfront. Once registered, you then need to give them details of every article you've had published, something that can be done online. For the published article to be accepted it needs to have appeared in a publication with an ISSN: International Standard Serial Number. Many magazines print these (in small print) on the page where the editorial contact details appear in the magazine, although collecting agencies often have a database you can search to find this information.

Publication needs to have occurred relatively recently, within a couple of years (check the current guidelines on their website at www.alcs.co.uk), so it's a good idea to register as soon as you've had your first piece accepted. I record on my database the date I log the article publication with ALCS so that I know I've claimed for it.

While ALCS looks after the words, there's a similar scheme in operation for photographs. Operated by DACS in the UK (The Design and Artists Copyright Society - www.dacs.org.uk), their scheme works slightly differently in that you don't have to tell them about every photo you've had published, but you do need to keep a record of how many photos you've had published in total, and in how many different magazine issues … cue another bit of information to record on a database. I should point out that you can only claim for photos that you've taken, not anyone else's the magazine has used to illustrate your article.

The DACS claim system is called Payback, and you don't have to be a member to claim. You simply submit a claim online during their claim period. This usually takes place between July and the beginning of September, but check out their website for up to date details. Once you've made a claim they'll email you when it's time to submit another claim. Payments are usually made towards the end of the year. This is another reason why I say offering photographs can generate more income for you. Not only might magazines pay more for your articles, but you can claim secondary rights through DACS too.

Keeping records is therefore vital if you want to ensure you can claim all the money for your published articles that you are entitled to.

Chapter Sixteen

Upon Publication

Hooray! Your article has been accepted and, if you're lucky, you have been sent a free copy of the issue containing your article. Enjoy the moment of seeing your name in print and then chuck it to one side, yes? No. There are a few steps you should take first.

Getting A Copy

Not all magazines provide you with a free copy of the issue that your piece appears in. It's useful if they do, because it is usually sent to you a few days before the issue appears in the shops. There have been times when I haven't been aware that an article had been accepted and the first I've known about it is when a free copy of the magazine has dropped through the letterbox. This is rare, though.

A publication will try to advise you when your article will appear. This may come in email format directly from the editor, or the accounts department may issue a remittance slip detailing payment and when the article will appear. (More on invoicing shortly.)

Some magazines have stopped issuing free copies. There is a cost involved. Whilst the actual free copy of the issue may be a negligible cost to them, popping a physical copy in the post is getting more and more expensive. Some publications I work for now send a PDF version of the pages my piece appears on. In some ways, this is better, because it helps me out. This is because whenever I have a piece published I …

Scan It To Create An Electronic Copy

This usually means tearing the pages out of the issue so I can get them into my scanner. Why do I do this?

1. Having an electronic copy of a published article is useful when pitching new ideas to editors - particularly those who've never come across my work before. For example, if I was pitching an idea to a travel magazine about fun family holidays in Spain, and I'd already had an article published in another publication about Spain, or family holidays in France, then attaching a copy of that published article helps demonstrate that I know about this subject matter, and have experience of writing similar material. Sometimes, I've pitched an idea and an editor has come back and asked to see samples of my work, so I've emailed across a couple of suitable scanned pieces. (I scan them into PDF format because this is easily opened on most computers.)
2. If I've interviewed anyone in the process of creating the article, I like to send them a copy of the finished piece that their quotes appear in. Emailing an electronic copy is easier, and cheaper than sending them a physical copy.
3. It's useful to have a library of your published material, and storing it electronically may be easier than keeping physical copies. This library of work is useful to browse through at those times when every pitch you send off comes back with a rejection, and you begin to doubt your capabilities. At least you have a body of work to remind yourself that you can write publishable articles. You've done it before, so you can do it again. And sometimes, flicking through your published pieces can spark off new ideas.

The next step is to sit down and read your article, or rather, read what the editor has decided to publish of your article.

Compare Versions

When an article has been accepted for publication, you have little control over what actually happens to the finished piece. Editors can edit your text, cut it if there is a more pressing need for some of the space they'd allocated to your text, or rewrite some of it. At first, you may be alarmed by this, but don't be. Remember, editors are the experts of their publications. They know the style and their readership inside out. And they also have the responsibility of putting together the magazine to create a product that sells advertising space.

You might worry that an editor could change your article so much that the facts get distorted. It's rare. I don't worry about it, because it's never happened to me. I'm not saying that it never happens anywhere around the world, but it's never happened to me.

But sitting down and looking at the printed version compared with the final version you submitted can be a useful exercise. I take a highlighter pen to my version and highlight where changes have been made. What differences do you see? None? Brilliant! But if there are some differences, then take a moment to consider them.

- Ask yourself - why was this changed? Is the text improved? Does the message in your sentence come across more succinctly? Or is it clearer.
- Has the editor focused on one particular area of the text? The beginnings are one area I've noticed some editors like to titivate. Use it as a learning opportunity. When I had a column in *Country & Border Life* I spotted that the editor was always rewriting my opening paragraphs. I obviously wasn't getting them right. Over a couple of months I spotted the style they were applying - of setting the scene and revealing

what all of my senses were experiencing. After that moment, I ensured my articles all began in a similar way, and the editor commented that they appreciated I had changed my style. After that, I rarely saw any changes being made to my text.

- Is everything still in the same order? Sometimes editors might change your paragraphs around. I've never experienced this with articles that I've written in a journey-format, but for those Ten Top-type pieces I've seen a few amendments. Sometimes the two most extreme points get moved: one to the start and one to the end, as if the editor wanted to start with a bang and end with one too.
- Often it has nothing to do with your writing. Your article may appear in a different order because of the way that other page furniture has been laid out across the page.
- Compare titles and sub-headings. Has the editor used your title and subheadings, or have they been changed? Do you like what the editor has done? (Tough luck if you don't.) But can you see why the editor has changed it? Are the sub-headings in the same place?
- Has some information been updated? When editors hold onto material for a long time, some of the information you've used may become out of date. If an editor still wants to use your piece they may rewrite it to ensure that article is factually correct. For example, when I pitched an idea to the editor of a magazine about Dr William Penny Brookes, the man from the small Shropshire market town who helped get the modern Olympic Games movement going, I'd pitched the idea with a view to the piece being used in the issue when the Olympic games were running. But for some reason the editor didn't use it then. The piece appeared a few months later (when the topicality was no longer there in my opinion, but still

> - I'm sure the editor knew what they were doing). However, because I'd written the text assuming the article would appear whilst the games were running, any references to the games taking place in the present tense had been changed to the past tense. These changes were beyond my control, but at least the editor amended the article so it still made sense.

There will be some changes you spot that make no sense to you whatsoever. Without having that insider knowledge of the discussion that was going on in the editorial office at the time, some decisions just won't make sense. But on many occasions it is possible to learn from the changes. If you're keen on submitting more material to the same editor, then I would certainly encourage you to adopt any styles or preferences you see the editor applying to your work. Look at it as a useful third party critique of your work.

Invoicing

Publication is the time to ask whether an invoice needs creating, if you haven't done so already. Usually, an editor will tell you when they accept your article whether you need to submit an invoice, at what stage you need to invoice, and where you need to send invoices to. Some publications I work for ask me to submit the invoice at the same time that I submit the finished article. (This usually happens when I've pitched an idea to the editor and they've commissioned me to write it.)

Payment times for articles varies considerably. There are some publications that pay on acceptance, although these are few and far between. Some pay on publication, whilst others pay 30 days (or even 45 days, in some cases) after publication. Again, if you're keeping records of your submissions, it's worth making a note of when you expect to receive payment, so that you can start chasing it up when you need to. There are some publications (particularly the smaller circulation magazines) that enclose a cheque with your free copy.

It's worth bearing this in mind when you're pitching ideas and producing articles. We've seen that it's necessary to think several months ahead for some ideas. If you want to write a Christmas article, you may be pitching the idea in June. If the article is accepted you may have to deliver it by mid-October (for a monthly publication), if not sooner, and the article will then appear in the December issue, which is often published the month beforehand. If the publication pays in the month following the date of publication, that could mean you won't see payment until the end of January. That's some time difference between pitching the idea and doing the work and actually being paid for it.

If you're looking to generate an income from writing articles then understanding when you will be paid is important. The more articles you write the more chance there is of receiving something each month. It can take time to build up that level of work.

If a publication asks you to invoice them there is some specific information you need to include, but it's straightforward. You do not need any fancy software or special templates, although most word processor and spreadsheet software offer invoicing templates. I actually use my standard letter template, as if I were writing a letter, but I place the word INVOICE in capital letters near the top of the page.

Your invoice needs the following information:

- Your name and address. (Not only is this useful if they send payment by cheque - which some organisations still do, but their accounts department will need a supplier address for their records.)
- The name and address of the company you're invoicing - so it's clear who needs to pay up.

- The word INVOICE. You need to make it clear it's an invoice you're sending, and not a statement of account. Most companies only pay on receipt of an invoice, not a statement of account.
- The date. All invoices need to be dated. Many companies operate a policy of paying invoices so many days after the date of the invoice (traditionally 30 days, although sometimes 45 days).
- A unique reference number. This is so that if you submit several invoices to the same company and there's a problem, it's possible to identify the specific invoice you have a query with. If you write for a publication on a regular basis it's common to be sending them several invoices for exactly the same amount on a regular basis. A unique reference number identifies a specific invoice. Don't panic about this. You don't need a complicated system. I use the year and then a sequential number. So my first invoice in the year 2020 will be 20200001, the next invoice will be 20200002 and so on.
- State what you're invoicing for. Mention the title of the article, and if you know which issue the piece is appearing in, state that too. It can be useful to mention the name of the editor who accepted or commissioned the item. (That way, if accounts have a query they have a name to contact within their own organisation.)
- The amount. Obviously, a publication needs to know how much they have to pay you, but if they pay one fee for the words and another for the photos you're offering, then break this information down on the invoice. This can be important, because for internal budgeting purposes the publication may need to split your payment between the article budget and the picture budget.
- Sales Tax. In the UK you only need to register for VAT if your business generates a certain level of

income, which varies in each government budget, but for most writers it's not something to be worried about. If your writing is generating that much income then you probably have an accountant to deal with your work. If you are registered for VAT then your VAT registration number needs to be displayed prominently on your invoice.

- Payment options. List all the different ways the publication can pay you. Your name and address gives them the option to pay by cheque, but quote your bank account details so that payments can be made directly into your bank account. (Ideally, you should have a separate account for your writing income.) Remember that if you're invoicing a publication in a foreign country you may need to change the currency you're invoicing in, as well as quote any international references for direct bank payments. This may include an IBAN or Swiftbic code. This information should appear on your bank statement. Some publications are happy to pay by PayPal, so quote the relevant PayPal address. (Again, having a specific PayPal address for your writing income can help keep things separate from your personal finances.)

These days, most invoices are emailed, so what I do is save it in PDF format, which ensures that anybody can open it no matter what computer system they use.

Chasing For Late Payment

It's easy to think that big businesses are trying to rip you off when payment isn't forthcoming. Again, in the vast majority of cases you'll be paid when you are due. I know from many writer friends that when payment doesn't arrive it's usually because they've not understood when exactly payment should be made, rather than there being any conspiracy by the publication.

Make a note of when payment should be made, but don't chase when it is 24 hours late. If the money hasn't arrived after a couple of weeks, make gentle enquiries. Don't go to the editor. The editor rarely has much input into the accounts department, apart from confirming that an invoice should be paid, because they've commissioned the work. Go to the accounts department and ask whether they've received the invoice. Mistakes do happen. If they haven't, ask who you should send another copy to and when you can expect it to be paid. If you're told the next payment run is in a week's time, accept it, but make a note. If payment is not forthcoming then, chase up the accounts department again.

If payment is still not forthcoming, then it might be worth dropping the editor a polite email, enquiring if they're able to help you. Remember, this isn't personal, it's a business transaction. Explain that you've had difficulty in obtaining payment and enquire if there is anything they can do to help move things along.

In the UK, the Late Payments of Commercial Debts (Interest) Act 1998 entitles small businesses (which includes freelance writers) to charge interest on late payments. Currently, business can charge an interest rate of 8% plus the current Bank of England base rate, so if the base rate is 2%, you can apply a 10% late payment interest charge, for the number of days late the payment is. So, if your outstanding invoice of £100 was 45 days late, and the Bank of England base rate was 2% you can charge the following:

Initial Invoice Amount: £100

Late Payment Interest of 10% (2% base rate plus 8%) = £10)

Divided by 365 days to get a daily interest rate of £0.027

Multiplied by 45 days = £1.23

Total Invoice, Including Late Payment Interest = £101.23.

It's worth checking the up-to-date legislation online, because there have been several amendments to this act over recent years, and you'll also be able to find out what the current late payment interest rate is.

I've only ever had a problem with payment once, and I was lucky in that I'm a member of a writing organisation that took up my case and arranged payment. However, the small claims court process in the UK is easy to follow and can be the best way forward if payment is running months late.

Of course, once you start encountering real difficulties in getting payment, you need to question whether you should be submitting any more material to this publication. That's where getting in touch with the editor at the appropriate time can be useful. If the editor is keen for you to continue writing for them, they'll probably give the accounts department an appropriate rollicking. But if the editor can't help and you're having to resort to the small claims court, then its time to start looking for new markets.

However, I do want to end this on a positive note. As I said I've only ever had a real problem once in the last twenty years that I've been writing magazine articles. So it is not as big an issue as you might think it is. Yes, mistakes happen. Invoices get lost, or the editor is late authorising and submitting your payment and so it has to go into the next payment run. Nobody is perfect. But don't let an innocent mistake develop into something that ends up with you not writing for that publication ever again.

Make sure you update your records with having received payment, because you don't want to embarrass yourself chasing for a payment you've already received.

Ends

At the end of every article, put the word *Ends*. It sends a clear signal to the editor that there is nothing else to follow. When you consider the fact files and further information panels you might list after your article, and the list of photographs you're including with your submission, along with your mini-biography for the *This Issue's Contributors* section, there can be quite a lot of stuff that follows on after your article text. If you're sending a paper copy through the post it's surprisingly easy for the back page to be cast adrift somewhere. Mistakes can also happen when copying and pasting your text from your Word document into the body of an email for an electronic submission. So *Ends* at the end tells the editor they have your entire submission.

And now I've reached that point in this book. I hope you've found the information here useful and practical, and you are now inspired to write your own articles for publication. It can be done. It is an accessible market.

If you've enjoyed it, and especially if it has helped you get your first article published, then please drop me an email at contact@simonwhaley.co.uk. I'd love to know about your success.

The best way to improve your article writing skill is to write plenty of articles. And don't forget to read them too. We can learn a lot from how other writers put their articles together. I look forward to reading yours.

Best wishes,

Simon

Ends.

ABOUT THE AUTHOR

Simon Whaley has had over 600 articles published and is the author of more than a dozen books, including the bestselling *One Hundred Ways For A Dog To Train Its Human*. For more information about Simon, and to read more of his articles, visit his website at www.simonwhaley.co.uk

INDEX

active sentences	120, 121
adverbs	119, 120
ALCS - Authors Licensing and Copyright Service	193, 194
anecdotes	10, 20, 78
angles	11-13, 18-22, 51-52, 60, 74, 140-141, 145, 148, 160, 163-164, 172-173
anniversaries	12, 14-15, 61
article analysis	40
Artist's Way, The	79
Bayeux Tapestry	12,
BBC Countryfile	16, 46, 74, 80, 83, 94, 139
beginnings	60-61, 73-74, 76-77, 81, 85-86, 91, 144, 199
Benjamin Flounders	74-75
Berne Convention for the Protection of Literary and Artistic Works	176
Best of British	139
Bleak House	80
Box.com	133, 170
boxouts	46, 93-96, 133, 134
byline	31, 41, 82, 130, 171
Cairnryan	17
call to arms	88
Carers UK	90
Charles Dickens	80

chasing 149-151, 190-192, 204
Choice 28, 29
chronology 60
circular structure 87-88, 90
Clive Owen 13
contents page 29-31, 48, 96, 99, 139
contributor biography 31, 96, 207
contributor photograph 96, 99
contributors 16, 31, 96, 99, 207
copy.com 133
copyright 135, 176, 183-185, 191
Copyright Licensing Agency 193
Country & Border Life 77, 86, 89, 143, 199
Country Living 28, 36
Country Walking 8, 13, 37, 42, 48, 59, 78, 83, 87, 89, 98, 147
creative non-fiction 101-116

DACS – The Design Artists Copyright Society 194-195
Derbyshire 18
Derbyshire Life 18
dialogue 76-78, 89, 102, 109-113, 122
Dogs Monthly 29
Dogs Today 29
double spacing 154, 157-159
Dr William Penny Brookes 75, 200
Dropbox.com 133
Dylan Thomas 12

Eardisley	80, 134
earthquakes	15, 18, 78, 88, 112
editing	117-127, 129, 154, 155
editor, at large	142
editor, commissioning	31, 143
editor, Deputy	31, 143
editor, Features	31, 143
editor, Section	143-144
editorial changes	48,
editorial contacts	29, 39, 142-143
Elizabeth Taylor	12
endings	68, 85-92, 173
Evernote	7
exclusivity	180, 183
expert quotes	46, 90, 109
Fishguard	10-13, 15, 17, 19-20
Fishguard Tapestry	12
Flesch Reading Ease	123
Flesch-Kincaid Grade Level	123
formatting	153-161
Freelance Market News	76
Freshen Up Your Fishpond	5
front cover	24-29, 61, 136
further information sections	3, 93-96
Goodwick	11
headlines	26-27, 124

Holyhead 17, 19
human interest 5, 18-20

I'll Sleep When I'm Dead 13
ideas 7-20, 51, 80, 97, 140-141, 176, 198, 202
International Space Station 99
interviews 67-68, 111-113, 171
invoicing 201-206
ISSN - International Standard Serial Number 194

Jemima Nicholas 12
journalistic questions 3-4
journeys 64-67
Julia Cameron 79, 88
justification 157

keeping records 148-149, 189-195, 201

Lakeland Walker 8, 97
late payments 204-206
Late Payments of Commercial Debts (Interest) Act 1998 205
letters 37, 47, 61, 63, 91, 155, 161
logical sequence 69-72
looking forward 90

margins 153, 157

market analysis	21-49, 59, 68, 73-74, 81, 94, 96, 139-142, 151, 163, 173
media packs	38-39, 40
Microsoft Word	123, 160
Moby Dick	12
Morning Pages	79, 88
Much Wenlock	75
MultiMarkdown	159
National Union of Journalists	175
news story	2, 4, 103
non-fiction, literary	102
non-Fiction, narrative	102
non-fiction, new journalism	102
non-fiction, reality fiction	102
non-fiction, The art of	102
non-fiction, the art of fact	102
numbers	15, 61-62, 126
Olive	28
Olympic Games	75, 200
One Hundred Ways For A Dog To Train Its Human	65, 98
Outdoor Photography	41, 99
outline	51-57, 59-60, 73, 117-118, 145-146, 160
page furniture	93, 129, 200
paragraphing	157, 158
passive sentences	120-124

Pembrokeshire 66-67
pet phrases 122
Photocopy 193
photographs 8, 37, 96, 98-99, 129-137, 148-149, 174, 191, 194

Photography for Writers 129, 130, 191
pilcrow 156
pitching 32, 51, 139-152, 163, 198, 202

Pocketmags 24, 178
point of view 102-103, 113
Public Relations agencies 135
primary source 103-104, 114-116
problem page 37-38
pseudonym 171-172

Q&A 67-69, 72
questions 3, 67-72, 78-79,108, 114, 117-118, 142

quotes 46, 76, 89, 93, 102, 109, 112

readers' letter page 37, 47
readers' photos 37
readership analysis 33-40
reviews 95
Richard Burton 12
rights 175-187, 189, 193-195

rights, all 183
rights, electronic 178, 182, 183
rights, first british serial 177-183
rights, first north american 178-183
rights, first worldwide serial 184-185
rights, secondary 193-195
Rosslare 11

Saga Magazine 35
scene setting 77-78
scenes 104, 107-109, 110, 199
sentence spacing 155
Shropshire 18, 74-75, 78, 80, 83, 97, 98, 200
side panels 93, 133
Society of Authors 175
socio demographic definitions 39-40
standard contracts 181, 184
standfirsts 41, 82-84
startling statements 74-76, 172
straplines 27-29
structures 30, 46, 55, 57, 59-69, 71-73, 86-88, 90, 104, 107-109, 118, 172-173
style 40-41, 43-44, 68, 77, 80, 122-123, 126, 159, 199-201

Take A Break 38-39
templates 47, 154, 202
tense 126, 201
The Lady 15, 18

The People's Friend	35-36, 41, 66-67
The Simple Things	79, 87
The Sunday Times Travel Magazine	28, 29
There Goes (Varoom Varoom) That Kandy-Kolored Tangerine-Flake Streamline Baby	101
time	63
titles	40-41, 81-83
Tom Wolfe	101, 114
topical hooks	14-16, 52, 80
tourist boards	131, 135, 164
travel	5, 8, 23, 30, 64-66, 76, 94, 102, 113, 131, 135, 143
Uncommon Waters	165-170
Under Milk Wood	12
unsolicited	32, 139-140
Waterways World	82
Willings Press Guide	1
word count	42-43, 47, 96, 117, 122, 123, 127, 171
word length	42, 141
Writers' Guild	175
Writers' Forum	79
writing for free	185-187
Writing Magazine	48, 82, 86, 90, 145, 147, 152
Zinio	24, 178

Made in the USA
Charleston, SC
09 January 2015